Freedom

Is More Than Just A Seven Letter Word

a book by Veronica: of the Chapman family

Free**M**an-**O**n-**T**he-**L**and

First Edition: September 2009
Second Edition: September 2010
Final Edition: September 2025

This book is all about freedom. I think it will surprise you how much you actually do not know about that subject. And how very little, in essence, you really need to know in order to attain it.

I hope that, by the time you have read it all the way through, your path into the future will be obvious to you. You should discover that, even at the age of 7 years old, you had more power than any Government, Judiciary, Police Force and Military combined. But you did not realise it. And therefore, throughout your life, you have thrown it away. But take heart, it is still there. And you can learn how to use it.

After having read the Chapters on *Taking* and *Money*, you may be wondering why you paid a price for a copy of this book. The answer is pretty obvious. The Monetary Belief System is still 'king', however much one would wish it away. Suffice to say, the majority of that price was the production, printing and any postage costs. As the Author, my royalty has been reduced to the barest minimum, in order to keep down the overall cost. Consequently, in that respect, it forms a labour of love on my part.

What is worth more than all the gold in the world is your appreciation that, having read this book, you have become empowered in the way you always should have been - had you been educated, rather than indoctrinated - during your childhood.

I apologise, up front, for the use of word-stressing in the text of this book. I'm compelled to do that in order to attempt to overcome the ingrained indoctrination to which we have all been subject throughout our lives. And the lives of our ancestors living or now deceased. I only have 'the printed word' (in its various forms) at my disposal.

Please also note that, if you wish, you may quote any part of this book under one restriction only: That you quote exactly **as is and within context** ... because I cannot be held responsible if you should misquote me. One final thing. Please don't worry about the grammar or the style. It's written exactly the way the Author wanted it written. I know that, because I'm that Author.

Veronica: of the Chapman family,

September 2009, Feltham, UK.

Preface to the 2nd Edition

It is now a year since the First Edition was published. A lot has happened in the interim, but very little (if anything) that seriously detracts from what was written in that First Edition. Which is why (typographical errors, and other minor corrections aside) the First Edition still stands 99.999% as originally published. And, therefore, this Second Edition simply adds to the catalogue of what we now know.

In the intervening year, letter after letter has been written by myself and many others. All told, there must have been thousands written. I have never once seen a ***substantial*** reply to any "Freeman" letter. And that's when a response has actually been forthcoming. When letters requesting clarification are sent, 'ignoring us' (as if – that way - we will just 'disappear') seems to be the order of the day. (Yes … childish).

So there you have it: 'They' can't answer straightforward and sensible questions, and consequently lose the arguments by default. Interestingly, NatWest wrote to someone explaining that *"... they reserved the right NOT to respond to his letters"*. It was pointed out that, if one emulates an ostrich, it's a good idea to remember which part of one's anatomy is most exposed.

So what are we to make of that? Surely it has become (somewhat painfully) obvious that 'minions' really don't have a clue? If they write back at all, it will be from templates. 'By rote', because that's all they know how to do. What they write doesn't make any kind of straightforward, reasonable, or logical sense. They write everything from the robotic standpoint of ignorance ***and arrogance***.

Thus the conclusion is obvious: It really doesn't matter what you write to them. It certainly doesn't make any substantial difference in the whole scheme of things.

But we have discovered the keys. THE keys. And you'll find them here - in this Second Edition. They are 'Sovereignty' (YOUR sovereignty) and 'their' Oaths of Office. Understand these keys, and I firmly believe you unlock Pandora's Box to your Freedom.

In order to keep the whole thing balanced I have added all the additional thoughts and findings into a new Appendix called 'Updates creating the 2nd Edition'. Thus you can now read the basics (as before), and then supplement that knowledge with what is contained in the Second Edition Appendix.

Veronica: of the Chapman family,

August 2010, Feltham, UK.

Preface to the Final Edition

First of all I wish to make an apology. References to WebSite www.FMOTL.com no longer work. (The site still exists, but is owned by some Americans – at the time of writing – and they have no connection whatsoever with myself, nor with this book).

So, unfortunately, I'm just going to have to apologise for the references that no longer work. The important reference was to the Templates, referred to in this book. They are still available online, via Google.

1. Go to YouTube Channel for **Cassie O'Calculator** (that's me).
2. Select video ***Channel Introduction***.
3. Underneath the video itself, click '***more***' to expand the text. You will find a link to a .ZIP file of the Templates, with a URL that enables them to be downloaded from Google Drive.

The remainder of the information in this book is pretty accurate, and still well worth reading and knowing, since it stands on its own two feet, without necessarily requiring the Website linkages.

Secondly, it may be necessary to point that the techniques suggested in this book are ***not*** designed to "*get away without paying for things*"! The techniques in this book are designed to **prevent you from being robbed**.

Thirdly, in this book I refer to the original Magna Carta, signed by King John, under duress, in 1215. However there were two more issues: one in 1216, and a further issue in 1225, by King Henry III. In the 1225 issue, the phrase "***of our own spontaneous goodwill***" is employed, to emphasise that it is issued willingly, and not under any kind of duress. The important Articles 39 & 40 are retained as Article 29 in the 1225 issue, and thus that Article is perfectly valid: ***"No free man shall in future be arrested or imprisoned or disseised of his freehold, liberties or free customs, or outlawed or exiled or victimised in any other way, neither will we attack him, or send anyone to attack him, except by the lawful judgement of his peers or by the law of the land. To no one will we sell, to no one will we refuse or delay right or justice".*** See ***Magna Carta***, by Dr. David Starkey, pages 205 and 207.

Fourthly, all references to *High Courts*, includes Crown Courts.

UPPERCASE TEXT isn't "shouty". It's just a different emphasis.

Lastly, my other book is *Anarchy Is More Than Just A Seven Letter Word.*

I dedicate this book to everyone in the Freedom Movement, without whom (and without whose support) writing it would not have been possible.

You are heroes. You are heroines.

And you know who you are.

"Reason is the life of the law; nay, the common law itself is nothing else but reason. The law which is perfection of reason"

Sir Edward Coke, Lord Chief Justice of England 1552-1634.

"Corruption is not the problem. It's the ***acceptance*** *of corruption that's the problem"*

Patrick Rattigan ND.

"I just say what I say because everyone is entitled to my opinion"

Saffire: of the Elder family (aged 7).

I write this book for Yana, and Saffire, and all the little ones like them. And I thank Yana's mother for the cover design.

Contents

Foreword

I am not a Solicitor. I am not a Lawyer. I am not an Accountant. I am not an Economist. I am not, in any way 'legally-trained', nor am I qualified to pontificate on 'monetary or economic policy'. It is hoped that, if you read this book all the way through, you will be very glad I am none of those things.

So, what are my qualifications? Well, I have some academic ones (in engineering), but they are not directly relevant to the fundamental messages contained in these pages. They do provide me with a background in 'working things out', but that's all.

My fundamental qualification for writing this book, my primary one, is that I am a Human Being. Blessed with a living soul. Just like you. And that's the only qualification I need for writing this book, and the only qualification you need for reading it. And, I hope, for understanding it.

I believe I have Common Sense. I believe you do, as well. I believe that's all that's actually necessary. I believe that, by simply tapping into your Common Sense, we will end up in complete agreement.

I certainly hope so.

Everything stated in this book is either based on my own personal experiences, or on the experiences of people I know and trust. And it's all based on Common Sense anyway. It really is just the practical application of Common Sense, as you will see.

So where do we start?

Well, first of all I'd like to quote Mahatma Gandhi when he said: *"There is no path to peace … peace IS the path"*.

Is it, therefore, OK if I say: *"There is no path to freedom … freedom IS the path"*? I reckon it's OK to say that. Because it's true.

Whoa! What does that mean? Well it means that to be free - you have to be free. And nothing else will do.

I have devised a Very Cunning 2-Step Plan to achieve freedom. I expand on this in more detail, in a Chapter all of its own. But, fundamentally, the two steps are:

1. You are free because you say you are free. Because no-one else will say it for you.

2. The second step is to make sure everyone you encounter recognises Step One.

It sounds easy, but obviously it isn't. In fact even Step One is extremely hard because it takes a constant effort to hold the line. This line has to be held 24/7. For example, most people in the British Isles, will say: *"Of course I'm free! I live in a democracy, don't I? I have freedom of speech, don't I?"*

Well, the straight answers to that are: *"No"*, *"No"* and: *"No"*.

I'll add one more quotation, from 18th/19th century philosopher Johann Wolfgang von Goethe: *"Those most hopelessly enslaved are those who falsely believe they are free"*.

And that's the nub. Or maybe you could say, the rub. Is one's belief in one's freedom false or true? Is one really free, or hopelessly enslaved?

There's a pretty simple test. Do you think something… something that happens (or has happened) to you, is (or was) unfair? And you can't see how to put it right? It doesn't matter what it is … but: *"Did it happen to you, was it unfair, and was there very little you could do about it"*? If the answer to that question is: *"Yes"*, then you are hopelessly enslaved.

Hey! Don't worry! Plenty of that has happened to me! However, by the time you've read this book, I hope you will be in the position of knowing 'how to put it right'. (Not necessarily how you can right wrongs done to you in the past, but how to prevent wrongs happening to you & your loved ones in the future).

Because, generally speaking, we all understand the difference between right and wrong. We are built that way. It's called Common Sense. We just feel it, more often than not. But, just because we are only feeling it, doesn't mean that we can, or should, ignore such feelings.

Because within them lies the truth.

Listen: I'm anxious to get on with what I plan to say. And I'm sure you feel the same way. All fired up and raring to go! So, having laid just a little bit of groundwork, let's quickly move on to the first Chapter.

How does that sound?

OK, well just a couple of final things before we can do that, because I just need to say, in order to fully comprehend the purpose behind this book, the Reader needs to be familiar with the works of other writers, such as David Icke, Jordan Maxwell, (the late, great) William Cooper, Eustace Mullins and G. Edward Griffin etc. If you are not, then I suggest you make up for it as soon as you possibly can. Nevertheless it is assumed that you know, deep down in your soul, that: *"Something is wrong with the set-up"* into which you were born.

Writers such as David & Jordan & others explain what those 'somethings' are in very great detail. And, if you know what those 'somethings' are, then you'll fully understand why I'm writing this book. However, if you don't know what those 'somethings' are, then we will just have to soldier on as best we can. Regardless. And simply rely on your 'basic, gut, feelings'. (I think it will all work out in the end).

Perhaps the very first thing to do is to start at the beginning (always a good place, I've discovered!). It will probably be a little bit of a surprise, but the first thing I do is to analyse the word: ***"Take"*** (including its derivatives).

And the reason for that, as you will see, is that it all starts from there.

Chapter 1: Taking

Huh? Just 'taking' is wrong, isn't it? Taking is 'greedy', isn't it? People are wrong to just take! Scroungers, tax dodgers … the lot of 'em! I can't stand people who think it is OK to just take! What right do they think they have to do that? Fair's fair! And just taking isn't fair! I worked hard for what I have!

Errr … 'scuse me. Just a moment. Can I interrupt, just one moment? Please? Pretty please?

Thanks.

What was the first thing you did when you were born?

Most people will say: *"I screamed my head off, so my mother said!"*

Well, no way, I'm afraid. Before you could scream you must have **taken** a breath. And, what's more, you continue to **take** breaths throughout your entire life.

Does the atmosphere ever send you a bill? Such that you pay it - for all the breaths you **take**? It would be a bit of a nuisance if it did that, wouldn't it?

Do you drink water? Where does it come from? Do you expect to pay back the sky, for all the rainfall you **took** – and drank?

Where does the light & heat come from? Do you expect the Sun to be paid back for all the light and heat you **took** from it, throughout your life? Do you expect an invoice, from the Sun, to land on your doormat one fine day?

Where do you get your minerals from? Oh! The Earth! Yes, of course! Does The Earth send out invoices, asking for payment for all the minerals **taken** from it (in your name)?

Well, no. People and Companies send invoices, but the atmosphere, the Sun & the Earth don't bother doing such an absurd thing.

We take everything. **We have to**. **There is no other way**. The alternative is death.

And we are not alone in this. Every single life form – from the lowliest amoeba to the grandest specimen of Homo Sapiens (i.e. you), does the same thing. That includes all animals, fish, reptiles, plants … everything organic.

What, in point of fact, do we (life forms) give back? Waste. Sewage. Pollution. (I can't think of anything else, on the physical level. With the exception of pollution, we do, after taking, actually contribute to the Life Cycle of the planet, in terms of the carbon dioxide we exhale, the organic waste we excrete, and the waste materials we leave behind when we die. However the point is that we have to **take**, in the first place, in order to live). **There is no dishonour whatsoever in 'taking', <u>provided you do not take more than your fair share</u>.**

The dishonour comes – or at least came – when certain families (historically) elbowed their way to the front of the queue, thrusting all others out of their way, and said: *"THIS IS ALL MINE! Everyone else sod off!"* **<u>That's dishonour</u>**.

Taking just what you need, no more, no less, is fair, reasonable, right, just and honourable. Because your only other option is death.

Scroungers, eh? Well scroungers actually ask permission, generally speaking: *"Ere, mate, gissacupla quid, will ya?"* .... *"Cor, fanks, mate! You're a bloody diamond!"*

Now, sit back and imagine something. Imagine a world in which everyone (that's everyone!) **just took**. Just took what they needed, whenever they needed it. Just what they needed, no more, no less.

No, don't laugh. Try to imagine it. It's really important. It is what is going to set us free.

Here's a quick example. The Farmer grows wheat. The Miller just takes the wheat, and grinds it into flour. The Baker just takes the flour, and bakes it into bread. The Farmer and the Miller just take the bread and eat it. The Baker eats his own bread. All three survive.

Now that was a very simplistic example, just to make the point. Obviously one has to expand that example to encompass all walks of life, but that can be done. However, certain 'walks of life' – those that are not in any way productive, would disappear. They would become obvious under a 'moneyless' paradigm. (Basically it would be everyone who you currently accept, grudgingly, as: *"Well, I suppose they are just doing their job"*)

The fundamental point is: That example is precisely what is happening already. The only factor left out of that example was 'money'. Or should I say 'methods of payment'?

So, how would that work without 'money/payments'? Well it would, I can assure you. Once again, I'm having to leave the detail until later, because I don't want to overload your Common Sense at this point.

Just keep reading. This whole book. All will be explained.

Taking

All I want to achieve, at this point, is that Common Sense tells you there is no dishonour, nothing to be ashamed of, in taking whatever you need, because you have no alternative. That nature provides for everything you need, and there is no alternative to nature. And Common Sense tells you that the Farmer, Miller & Baker would survive in that example.

So I guess the next stage, in order to flesh out the situation in which we find ourselves, is to recognise three very powerful Grand Deceptions, which have together suppressed many people's ability to listen to their own Common Sense.

So, let's make a start with … with what? Well, we have three choices: '*Money*', '*Legalese*' and '*Religion*'.

They are all Grand Deceptions, so let's start with *Money*.

Chapter 2: Money

The first Grand Deception is 'money'. **It's an illusion**. But, my goodness, a powerful one! This is probably the hardest part to understand. So I am going to have to explain as carefully as I can.

Well, what is 'money'? Most people will think of a £10 or £20 note, and say: *"That's money of course!"*

And the problem is: That's not money, of course. They are just pieces of paper, with a design printed on them, and a splash of silver-coloured ink.

Fundamentally people know that, coinage is not 'worth' the 'value' stamped on it i.e. coins cost peanuts to make. And banknotes the same. Surely no-one really believes it actually costs £5 to create a fiver? Or £10 to make a tenner? And so on?

I plead to your Common Sense! I prostrate myself, and grovel, at the feet of your Common Sense!

So, if 'money' is 'not worth the paper it is printed on', what, exactly, is it worth?

Perhaps one answer to that can be gained by defining it. What is the definition of 'money'? Here's Chambers Online:

money: noun (plural in sense 1b and 4 monies or moneys) 1 a coins or banknotes used as a means of buying things; b any currency used as legal tender. 2 wealth in general.

Wrong! Let's see if a Law Dictionary can be of more help. Here's Black's 8th edition:

money: 1. The medium of exchange authorised or adopted by a government as part of its currency; esp. domestic currency <coins and currency are money> UCC1-201 (b) (24) 2. Assets that can be easily converted into cash <demand deposits are money> 3. Capital that is invested or traded as a commodity <the money market> 4. Funds; sums of money <investment monies>

Wrong! And, not only that, I love the way (4) defines money as 'sums of money'. That's known as a Circular Definition.

These are wrong because they define 'cash', not 'money'. That's the same thing, is it? Well then, how come there is always talk about: "... *heading for a cashless society*"? And the benefits of it? I've never heard any mention of: *"... heading for a moneyless society"* in the Mainstream Media. As you will see, if you read on, the 'moneyless society' is the one we need, and (I believe) we are going to get - for the simple reason that we can't go on for much longer under the absurd and preposterous illusion of money.

And far too many people are waking up to that. There are a number of very serious proposals for working 'moneyless societies', such as the Resource-based Economy proposed by *The Venus Project* and *Zeitgeist Movement* (Google them for more information).

My definition of 'money' is, I think you will find, a lot more accurate. Here's me:

money: Conveniently transportable tokens of Credit.

Isn't that the same thing, then? Absolutely not! Let's examine my definition.

Well, first of all, 'conveniently' and 'transportable' are adjectives. Therefore all they do is to limit the scope of the subject of the definition. Take 'red' as an example. If I said: *"All cars"*, then I would mean every single car on the planet. If I added the adjective 'red' as: *"All red cars"*, I would not be talking about cars of a different colour, I would only be referring to the red ones. But I would still be talking about 'cars'.

So, the adjectives do nothing more than limit the scope of the subject, which, in the case of 'money', is: 'tokens of Credit'.

Yes, 'cash' is nothing more than tokens. We have already seen, by Common Sense, that the coins and banknotes - the cash - is fundamentally worthless. It has no more value, in reality, than tokens for a Fruit Machine. Or Green Shield Stamps (if you can remember those). Perhaps Supermarket Vouchers is a more up-to-date example?

What is a 'token'? A token is something real, something substantial in this 5-sense reality, something that can be touched, held, felt … that stands in place of - in other words represents - something that cannot represent itself.

A table does not need a token to represent it. A table is real, and can represent itself. A chair likewise. And so on.

The thing that cannot represent itself is 'credit'. **Because 'credit' is nothing more than an idea. A concept. Imaginary. A belief.**

A belief that a Shopkeeper has, such that if he swaps some goods for a £10 note, then he can use that £10 note at a later date, to make a swap with someone else.

But this mechanism only works because everyone concerned believes it. (And only because of that)

I say again: Because they believe it. And where are beliefs kept? Yes, **in your head. In your brain. In your imagination**.

And that's the only place beliefs are kept.

So the idea that 'money' is real … is an illusion. A Monetary System is nothing more than a Belief System.

That's why, throughout the world, Belief Systems can be different. There was a time, not so long ago, when the Germans believed in deutschmarks, and the French believed in francs, and the British believed in pounds sterling.

At the time of writing the British still believe in pounds sterling, while the French and Germans now believe in Euros. **This is only possible with a Belief System**.

The British, French, Germans, Dutch, Italians, etc. all still know that a table is a table, and a chair is always a chair. And what to do with them. We don't need to believe in tables & chairs for that to be the case.

So, what is a banknote, or a coin? Well British banknotes give the game away, because they actually contain a printed promise. It goes like this:

"I PROMISE TO PAY THE BEARER ON DEMAND THE SUM OF …"… and then followed by the amount written numerically (known as the 'denomination' of the note, £5, £10, £20 for example).

(There is obviously not enough space for similar inscriptions on coinage).

What does this mean? **It's a promise**. Thus a banknote is a Promissory Note. A piece of paper containing a promise. And bearing the signature of whomsoever is making the promise.

Anyone in their right mind would call it an IOU!

So, the British are passing around IOUs, from the Bank of England, 24/7!

Do we ever expect the Bank of England to pay up, to make good, on their promise?

Actually, at least one person I know about, did try. The Bank of England quickly showed her the door (and called the Police!). Someone else I know tried the same thing at Barclay's. Once again she was also shown the door (which, by the way, was locked and bolted immediately after she left!)

Money

Well, if you think the Bank of England will make good on their promise, then feel free to try. I very much doubt you will succeed where others have failed, for the simple reason that the Bank of England cannot fulfill on a Belief System.

The Promissory Notes the British move around 24/7 are nothing more than empty, meaningless, IOUs.

And they call it 'money'. And wars are fought over it. People die, and are subjected to atrocities for it. People commit suicide over it. In point of fact just about every 'cide' (genocide, patricide, homicide, suicide, etc.) is committed in the name of empty, meaningless, promises.

IOUs by any other name.

This would all stop on the day that what I've written herein is recognised as the truth, and Common Sense.

Is it such a large step, by the way, to see how these empty, meaningless, promises can be converted to numbers in computer databases, and implants on plastic cards?

Furthermore is it such a large step to imagine that we could run a world quite well, without the need to sling empty, meaningless, promises all over the shop?

After all, the Euro notes don't even bother to make the promise, because the whole thing is so utterly worthless and superfluous. I'm fairly sure that, if the Bank Of England's notes said: *"I PROMISE TO PAY THE BEARER ON DEMAND 5 UNICORNS"*, and so on, people would start to cotton on. By saying: *"'Scuse me, but what the hell is the good of 5 mythical creatures?"* Well, of course, the Bank of England's current promises are actually mythical creatures.

People say: *"Without money, there would be no incentive for anyone to do anything"*. What a terribly myopic thought!? Try sitting around, doing nothing, for any period of time. I submit you would be climbing the walls looking for something to do.

Something constructive to do.

Well, you need to eat, don't you? So, at the very least you would need to: *"Get up off your bum, and go get some food"*. And the same for your children, etc. That may not be overly constructive to the good of the community in general, but it is an incentive. And it is an incentive that does not need to be triggered by money. (It's triggered by hunger)

Just about every example one can think of can be thought through rationally, in much the same way. It just needs to be thought about carefully, that's all. It is no good half-thinking. Only whole-thinking will return the correct conclusions.

Go back to the example of the Farmer, Miller & Baker. Why does that example need to include the necessity to hand around empty, meaningless, IOUs from the Bank of England, for that example to work?

When all they actually need to do, is to say: *"Sod it. We'll just do it!"* I think you'll find the reason is pretty obvious. The Farmer, Miller & Baker are in a real situation. Adding a component called 'method of payments' is only adding beliefs to that reality. This belief contributes nothing whatsoever to the actions taken by the Farmer, Miller & Baker. They could farm, mill & bake without any knowledge ... other than farming, milling & baking. Subtracting the beliefs from the reality is subtracting zero from the overall equation. Subtracting zero from either side of an equation leaves the resulting balance unchanged.

What's the difference between: *"I know it works. I can see it works. I think/believe it works this way"*, and: *"I know it works. I can see it works"*? Answer: *"Nothing. Both say exactly the same thing,* ***in fact****"*. It's just that, in the former case, the added belief may - **or may not** - be correct. But that doesn't matter, because it's only a belief, anyway ... **and therefore totally discardable**.

Duh! You don't need to barter, baby, you just need to 'do it' (honourably contribute)! Sheesh!

What right does some **private** banking cartel (the Bank of England) have to say only its empty, meaningless, promises are the ones to use? Why are its empty, meaningless, promises so much better than some empty, meaningless, promise of yours? Or better than those real promises the Farmer, Miller and Baker make to each other?

If the Farmer suddenly ups and says: *"No, you can't have any more wheat"*, then the Miller can say: *"In that case I can't make any flour, and the Baker can't make any bread, and therefore you won't have any bread to eat"*. That would not happen because it would be so blindingly obvious. Common Sense.

Money is an illusion. Based on empty, meaningless, promises from the Bank of England in the UK, and the Federal Reserve (yet another **private** banking cartel) in the US.

(If you are reading this somewhere else in the world, don't worry ... it's exactly the same where you are located. The Grand Deception, the illusion of 'money', is the same throughout the world). Who says so? Her Majesty's Treasury say so. In reply to a Freedom of Information Request I made. (See an Appendix for details).

Money

I'll be returning to this subject later, when I discuss *Mind Control and Enslavement.* Because the Monetary System is one of the primary mechanisms for Mass Mind Control and Enslavement.

However, in the meanwhile, here are a few things to consider in odd moments, as you may read on in this book.

Think about this.

Light. Where does it come from? It doesn't take much imagination to know that daylight comes from the Sun.

So, without going into to the deep science of the situation, we can freely say that: *"The Sun is the source of all our daylight".*

Heat. We can say a similar thing for heat that warms our planet. It comes from the Sun.

Water. That comes from the sky, drops as rain, and eventually evaporates back into the sky again. In a cycle. But where did the original water come from? Once again, no real science is involved in the answer. It has been there since the planet was formed.

The point of this explanation is: *"These things have an <u>ultimate source</u> ... for practical purposes, anyway".*

And a little thought says that everything must come from somewhere. Everything has to have an ultimate source, for practical purposes.

And so it must be that money has an ultimate source, does it not?

If so, what is that ultimate source? Have you ever thought about it?

Does it grow on trees? Does it come from the Sun? Does it drop like rainfall?

Well, no, it doesn't. Everyone understands that.

So where does it come from, then?

Ask anyone where their money comes from, and they will generally reply: "*I work, to earn it*". So you can then ask: "*But who gives it to you?*" and they will say: "*The Company I work for, of course!*"

Then you can ask: "*Where does the Company you work for get it from, so that it has some to pay over to you?*" and they will say: *"Well, they sell goods to Consumers, or they provide services to Consumers ... and they charge for it. So that's how they get their money".*

And so you can say: "*Well, where do these Consumers get their money from, so as to pay for these goods & services?*" and the answer will come back: "*Well, they work for other Companies ... who pay them for the work they do! Cor! Are you daft, or something?*"

So now we are just going round and round, aren't we? We have still not established the ultimate source of where money comes from, in the first place.

Probing a little deeper, an answer might be: "*My Company gets it from a Bank, I suppose*". So then it is possible to ask: "*Well, where does the Bank get it from, then?*"

And then you'll possibly get: "*Well, I suppose the Banks must make it … I don't know!*"

So you can then say: "*Well, if the Banks make it, then why do they expect you – if you take out a loan – to pay them back? I mean, if they can just make it anyway? And why did they need a bailout of it, in late 2008? And why did Banks go out of business, if they can just make money?*"

And you are very likely to end up with the retort: "*Well, I don't know! Ask them!*"

To which the obvious rejoinder is: "*Well, do you not think it would help you to know? Because, if you did – know where it came from, I mean – then maybe – just maybe – you could go and get some … to help you over any money problems you might have? Have you never had any money problems? Most people have. Do you not think that knowing where money actually comes from, in the first place, might help you?*"

The response will probably be: "*I dunno*".

And that's the point. **Who, precisely, knows where money actually comes from? In the first place?**

Who knows how it gets into circulation?

So let's look around for the possible sources.

My next door neighbour? No … he's in the same trouble as I am.

My employer? No … we've already been through that.

The Banks? Well, no … at least not most of them … but there is the Bank of England, and that doesn't go out of business, did not need a bailout, and its name is printed on every banknote. So they are a distinct possibility. Let's keep them in mind.

What about HM Revenue & Customs? No … they want money, so they can't be the source of it.

The DVLA? No … they also want money, so they can't be the source.

The Local Councils? No … they also want money.

The Government? Well, yes this is possible. But one of the Government Agencies is called HM Revenue & Customs, and they **want** money. So that's a bit strange, isn't it? Let's also keep that in mind.

Money

Now there is a Government Agency that never asks for money. I wonder if there is something in that? The Agency in question is located in Horse Guards Road, London. It is called HM Treasury.

Have you ever received a demand from HM Treasury? I haven't, in my entire life.

So how does HM Treasury operate, without demanding money with menaces?

That's a question, surely?

And it can be shown that the Bank of England is also a private Bank, just like RBS, HSBC, Barclay's, etc. So they should be in the same position, needing a bailout.

But, what the privately-owned Bank of England has, in its favour – which none of the others have – **is the ability to print money**.

A privately-owned Bank, with the ability to print money. That's an interesting situation to be in, of course.

But that's only printing it. It still doesn't explain how these printed notes, and minted coins, actually get into circulation.

We know that someone does not stand in Threadneedle Street, with a bucketful of it, and hand it out to passers-by. We also know that they don't hire an aircraft and bail it out, letting it float down to whomsoever can catch it.

But we also know that we never receive demands from HM Treasury, the Bank of England, nor the Royal Mint.

And we also know that we ***do*** receive demands from just about everyone else.

So, I think, we have some clues to suggest that money is created by HM Treasury, printed by the Bank of England in accordance with instructions from HM Treasury, and minted by the Royal Mint under similar instructions from HM Treasury. And that it is released into circulation via a mechanism we have not been told about (as yet).

Does anyone have a better idea?

Because money must come from somewhere, and I think I have eliminated most of the other possibilities.

So now lets turn to the 'strangeness' of HM Revenue & Customs. In conjunction with HM Treasury. They are both 'HM's, which stands for 'Her Majesty's', of course.

So, even if HM Treasury is not the ultimate source of money, some 'HM' must be.

Let's assume it is HM Treasury. (After all, what else is their job, then?).

So we would have HM Treasury ***making*** money, and HM Revenue & Customs ***wanting*** money. **So why can't these two 'HM's just get together ... and leave us all alone?**

Well, that's another question, isn't it?

And then we can add that one of the jobs of the US Treasury, embodied in the Act creating it, was to 'issue warrants for monies'. Or, to put it another way, to provide authority for the creation of US currency.

And then, add to that, the UK Currency Act defines the weights and measures for coins, and also provides for the Chancellor of the Exchequer to apply an upper limit as to how much currency can be authorised into circulation.

The biggest problem is that HM Treasury will not admit to any substantial role in respect to the 'creation of money'.

However, **when asked point blank, *HM Treasury will not go on the record denying it.***

So that's interesting as well, isn't it?

Why would they be so coy?

Listen: I'm sorry to bat on about this, but **some** Government Agency **must be** creating 'money'. Thus, if 'money' is required to pay for the (say) maintenance of roads, then surely there is nothing to stop the appropriate agency that creates 'money' from creating the 'money' to pay for the maintenance of roads. Is there?

I'm really sorry, but **why bother you & I?**

It's not a Government Agency creating 'money', you say? OK, well, that still doesn't alter the essential point: If 'money' is required, for the maintenance of roads, then whoever is maintaining the roads should obtain the 'money' from whoever creates 'money'.

For crying out loud, there is still no need at all to bother you & I. Is there?

It doesn't work like that? OK ... how DOES it work then? Why do I need to get involved with Road Tax? Pedestrians & cyclists use the roads all day and every day. They are not bothered with these things.

How many more ways can I say the same thing? How many more examples do I need to offer? Did you elect your Government to look after the roads, or did you elect it to make absurd and unrealistic demands on you? Did you elect it to make the 'money', and then ask you for it?

Honey, they **make** the 'money'! Why do they want it back in Road Tax, Sales Tax, Council Tax, Inheritance Tax or TV Licencing, etc? Unless … unless … gosh-an'-golly-gee … are YOU the one who makes all the 'money'? 'Coz that means everything in this little book is complete rubbish! But never mind … listen, darling, if that's the case: Can I have your address, please … because: *"DAAARLING! Where HAVE you been all my life? Yes, of course I love you. Yes, of course I mean it! You are tall, dark, handsome, debonair … you remind me of my father, and all that. No, the money has nothing to do with it … don't be silly!"*

On the other hand, on the off chance it's not you who is making all the 'money', then (*Oh … poo! I thought I was on to something there!*) we are back to square one, aren't we? And so, as a final rant in this Chapter, it might be interesting to consider 'what goes away' when 'the Belief System, the Illusion of Money, the totally unnecessary Utter Absurdity of Money, goes away'.

What does it take with it?

Stealing is the first thing. There is nothing to steal. Hoarding is another thing. There is no point in hoarding, any more than there is any point in stealing anything. 'Sell', 'buy', 'value', 'commerce', 'exchange', 'barter', 'interest', 'wages', 'salary', 'debt' no longer have any meaning. And so on.

The Global Elite (see their own Chapter) are now seen to be as worthless as they - in point of fact - always were. Their Swiss Bank Accounts now count for nothing whatsoever.

Goodbye to the Stock Markets. Goodbye to the Banks. Goodbye to the Loan Sharks. Goodbye to the Debt Collectors. Goodbye to the Bailiffs, and the Accountants. And the Economists. *"Services no longer required"*. And so on.

'Rich' now becomes 'rich in good friends'. 'Rich in honour'. 'Rich in integrity'. And so on. Just like it always should have been. Just the way Common Law dictates.

All these imponderables are wrapped up, 'i's dotted, 't's crossed, in the final Chapter *Mass Mind Control & Enslavement*. But please don't skip to it. There's a lot more in between. By the time you have read this book all the way through, I think you will be in possession of a complete set of the most probable answers to all these questions. Answers that fit, what we all know to be true, like the pieces of a perfect jigsaw puzzle. Including the mechanism for releasing money into circulation in a controlled manner, and why everyone concerned would be so coy about the roles they play.

Chapter 3: Legalese

I'm going to discuss the English version of Legalese. Every nation on the planet will have its own version. (For reasons which, I hope, will become obvious). The same discussion and comments will apply. Because there is no other way.

Legalese is the language of Statutes. It is assumed that Statutes are 'the Law'. They are not, as you will see if you keep reading. Statutes are discussed within their own Chapter.

For now, I simply want to confine the discussion to Legalese itself. To show that it is an illusion. Another arm of the Grand Deception.

There is an old Roman Law maxim that states: *"Let he who will be deceived, be deceived".*

That is so, so true.

What, exactly, is Legalese? Well, first of all it is a language. It looks like English (in the British Isles), but it is no more 'English' than is any Foreign Language. French, for example. Or German. Or Croatian.

It is written by those who draw up Bills for Parliament (and Congress). It is assessed by Committees. It is voted on by Members of Parliament (or Congress). If agreed it becomes an Act of Parliament (or Congress). It becomes so-called 'law' when it receives the Royal (or Presidential) Assent. At that point it becomes a Statute. A Statute written in Legalese. A Statute written in a Foreign Language.

Now, you may be forgiven for asking: *"How can I be expected to obey a rule written in a Foreign Language? How can I even be expected to understand what I am supposed to obey as an upright, law-abiding, citizen?"*

I, personally, would forgive you for asking that. Those who won't, are Members of your Government, the Judiciary - in terms of Judges, Clerks, Solicitors, Lawyers, Barristers, and Policemen. And the vast majority of your fellow Countrymen, quite probably including your own family & friends. And also including the Media.

But I would forgive you, because you would be exactly right. And so, I think, would any other sane, rational, honest, honourable and decent Human Being. Really anyone still capable of using even just a grain of Common Sense.

Legalese

Apart from being a Foreign Language (I'll explain why), it also comprises a number of fictions. As we all know 'fiction' is not the truth. 'Fiction' is not the reality (I'll explain this, as well)

Legalese is a Foreign Language because it re-defines or expands the meanings of certain words. English words. It does this for its own convenience (not yours, that's for sure!). One good example (I'll give you a better example in a minute) is the word 'understand'. Legalese expands this to mean 'stand under' - specifically (as we will see): *"Stand under, i.e. consent to, Legalese"*. So what does this mean? It means that if a Policeman, or anyone in a Court, asks you: *"Do you understand?"*, and you say: *"Yes"*, then you are agreeing to consent to the application of Statutes drafted in a Foreign Language. (Legalese is nothing if not thoroughly incestuous!).

Here's the real dooley: In Legalese the word 'person' is re-defined by expansion. The word 'person' still means what you and I would expect it to mean viz: a Human Being; But in Legalese it is expanded to mean: '... any grouping of people, any Partnership, any Company/Corporation'.

(I think those who drafted this standard for their own convenience, were assuming that they could move a word defining a singular, into a plural ... taking their cue from the fact that some English words are like that. 'Sheep' and 'fish' are obvious examples. However, I'm only guessing, and why they thought they could get away with it doesn't matter anyway).

The idea was, of course, to give Corporations, Companies & Societies the same or similar 'rights & duties' as a Human Being. An utterly stupid idea, as I hope you will appreciate, by the time you have read and fully-comprehended this book.

So, let's use some Common Sense to look into the sanity of expanding the definition of the word 'person'.

A Human Being has a head within which there is a brain, within which there is - what we would call - a Mind. And a Human Being is 'aware', is conscious, and has a soul. A Human Being also has eyes, and ears, and limbs. And so on.

A group of people, taken as a group, has none of these things. The individuals that form the group do (of course), but not the group - **of itself i.e. when taken as a 'legal entity' in it's own right.** It does not matter how much Legalese would like to grow arms & legs on a group, it cannot happen. It is physically impossible.

A simple example is 'deciding to do something'. A Human Being can work out what to do (using the brain), and do it, using its limbs. A Corporation has to firstly, go through the motions of making a collective decision, and then get/persuade/task a Human Being (e.g. an Authorised Company Representative) to actually do whatever has been decided.

More specifically, signing a document. A Human Being has limbs with which to grasp a pen, and a brain to control the necessary hand movements, in order to make his or her unique 'mark'. A Company has to fall back on tasking a representative to make a 'mark' ... on behalf of the Company.

When it comes to liability for actions taken, a Human Being can be fairly and squarely placed in the frame. In the case of a Company, buck-passing is the order of the day. Don't expect any Human Being, who is a part of any Company, to own up to anything!

Consequently, by no stretch, would any sane individual consider a single Human Being to be equivalent to a Group.

And that's where Legalese starts. It starts with insanity and irrationality ... and then steadily gets worse. It layers fiction (calling a Company as 'person') upon fiction. It creates what is known as a Legal Fiction Person from each and every Human Being. It does this in order to be able to fictionally equate a Human Being to a 'single-individual-partnership-or-CORPORATION' for 'legal purposes'.

This is done so that any adjudication in a Court de facto (what that means is explained later) is One CORPORATION .vs. Another CORPORATION. Very simply because it is perfectly obvious that no adjudication is possible between **the reality** of a Human being and **the fiction** of a CORPORATION.

How can anyone ever adjudicate between a reality and an illusion? The reality, the Truth, would always win against the fiction, the Untruth, hands down!

A Chapter in this book is devoted to *Legal Fiction Persons.*

It is also interesting to note that there is an excellent video available, called *The Corporation.* This video not only explains how and why CORPORATIONs all came about, but goes further to compare the actions of any CORPORATION to that of the real Human Being it purports to impersonate.

The video goes into massive detail in order to explore this concept. And, for that reason, it is highly recommended viewing. And what does it conclude? ***It concludes that, if a CORPORATION (any CORPORATION) were a real person, it would be a psychopath.***

And, furthermore, the definitions change from time to time. That's why Black's Law Dictionary is now in its 8th Edition (at the time of writing).

Legalese

Its 8th Edition of pure fantasy and absurdity.

You want some more? I'm reliably informed that if you look up 'Human Being' the 4th Edition of Black's Law Dictionary, you'll find the definition says: *"**See 'monster'**"*. This reference is removed by the time we get to the 8th Edition, of course. ***It's a moving carpet***.

Of course it is perfectly possible to step back and use a bit of Common Sense. The very fact that Law Dictionaries are necessary, gives the biggest hint. In English we already have dictionaries to define our language, in terms of normal parlance. The Oxford English is probably the best known, but there are many others. They do not define the word 'person' as a Corporation.

Because Legalese is a Foreign Language it needs its own dictionary. If it were not a Foreign Language it would not. Languages always need a dictionary. If we could always rely on Oxford English then we would, would we not? What would be the point of Oxford English otherwise?

Legalese is an illusion. A fictional world created for the benefit of mind control and enslavement. **It is an English look-alike**, and no more than that. Because it 'looks like English', no-one complains.

But we should. We should all complain. We should all say: *"This is bloody ridiculous! How dare you impose rules to be obeyed when they are written in a Foreign language? Get outta here!"* As you will see later, in the Chapter discussing *Promises & Contracts*, the vast majority of the so-called 'Legal Profession' have not the slightest clue about all this. Which means that if you understand the illusion of Legalese, then you can run rings around them.

I've got an idea! Let's dump Legalese on the Rubbish Tip of History, and stick to Oxford English, shall we? Then we'd all know where we stood, wouldn't we?

I have seen many examples of letters from Solicitors, Lawyers, and so-called 'Legal Scholars', which are a complete mass of double-think. Under careful and critical scrutiny just about anything they write can be shown to be totally contradictory, and thoroughly irrational. The reason for this is because they live in a fictional world, and are always attempting to replace Common Sense with fiction. They achieve little other than disappearing up their own hindquarters.

The benefit to you is that you can write plain commonsense, and they will not understand! They will not understand because Common Sense does not compute in their fictional, illusory, world.

Because they do not understand they will resort to ignoring what you said, and reply to the-question-they-wanted-you-to-ask. And they will reply in their own way. (How often do Politicians do that? How about like: *"Always"*? It's the same old smoke & mirrors). What this means is that they have 'not responded in substance' to the points you made. They could not 'respond in substance' because that would not compute with their illusion.

Since they have 'not responded in substance', they have dishonoured, and you have not. In Law: *"He who dishonours, loses"*.

Generally speaking, when it comes down to brass tacks, we have found that - for all their huffing & puffing - they **never** actually go to Court. Primarily (we think) this is because - at the end of the day - they know, deep down, that your Common Sense trumps their Legalese. Hands down.

One of the biggest questions to arise is: *"What's the difference between 'legal' and 'lawful'?"* Well here is one big clue. 'Legal' refers to the illusory world of Legalese.

'Lawful' means truly bound by Law (long established customs & traditions), in the real, Common Sense, world. The Law established over centuries, by consent (*Consensus facit legem* in Latin – *Consent makes Law* in English). There is much more about this later.

"Let he who will be deceived, be deceived". Don't be deceived.

Chapter 4: Religion

Religion is the third of the illusory triumvirate. People wrongly equate 'spiritual' with 'religious'. Whereas 'religion' is no such thing. Religion comprises dogma. For example to tell you that you need to be 'saved'. And how to be saved.

When, in point of fact, you need to be saved from three things only: 'Money', 'Legalese', and 'Religion'.

The imposition of religious dogma is designed to suppress your ability to use Common Sense. No? Well it does. In order to follow a religion - any religion - you have to be prepared to double-think, to a greater or lesser degree.

Double-thinking is the antithesis of Common Sense, and any critical thought processes based on Common Sense.

'Religion' is the third arm of the mind control and enslavement paradigm. Be as religious as you want. But don't forget that freedom is freedom. Even if you become free, with the help of later material in this book, is there any point in then surrendering any of your gains to any religion?

Once you know what you are, you don't need anyone else to tell you.

If religion is so empowering, why has no religious person (to the best of my knowledge) ever written this book? Or anything like it? Are you suggesting that plain unvarnished Truths, contained within plain old Common Sense, aren't worth preaching **loud & clear** from every pulpit?

Gosh, no. Religious dogma is far more important, isn't it? You have all the power necessary to save yourself & your loved ones.

But no ... don't do that ... let Jesus do it.

Reading Zecharia Sitchin's book *The 12th Planet* explains exactly how we all came to be here, and what 'God' is. Sitchin is an expert on the Biblical Old Testament, is fluent in Hebrew, and can read the original Hebrew versions of Ancient Texts. He explains how 'God' occasionally moves into the plural – i.e. 'Gods' – by referring to 'we' and 'our', etc.

These are possibly transcription mistakes from the Truth contained in the Ancient Sumerian Tablets. Or they could very well be deliberate mistakes, left in by the Ancient Scribes (who were quite probably re-writing history at sword-point), and left in by design, in order to give later readers 'a clue that all was not exactly as transcribed'. One does not know.

One cannot know. But Sitchin has picked them all up, and we all owe him a debt of gratitude for that.

In the Chapter on *Mass Mind Control & Enslavement* I explain the results of being created by these 'Gods' (the Biblical Nephilim). And how we would have taken their word for the way to live, and why we would have emulated them in all respects.

Yes, I know Sitchin has been 'outed' as one of the Reptilians. (The shape-shifters). In fact the information in his books, known collectively as *The Earth Chronicles*, could surely have only come from that kind of deep knowledge. The information, the insights and the critical thinking behind them, are far and away too consistent to be purely intuitive. His ideas are imparted with mathematical precision.

Sitchin is undoubtedly (in my mind at least) one of the few who are on Humanity's side.

According to the Ancient Sumerian Tablets, 'taxation' was rife in Ancient Sumer. 6,000 years ago.

Jesus (if he existed): *"Threw the moneylenders out of the Temple"*. According to the Bible he was once asked about taxation. His reply was: *"Render unto Caesar that which is Caesar's, and to the Lord that which is the Lord's"*.

It's a pity none of these people ever used a modicum of Common Sense, pointing out that 'money' is an illusion.

So it's now time to stand up and see how we have all been deceived for some 300,000 years. And re-claim our Humanity.

Chapter 5: Global Elite/Psychopaths

So we have three major illusions: *Money*, *Legalese* and *Religion*. All three deliberately designed for mass mind control and mass enslavement. So who is running this show?

Well, the best answer anyone has yet come up with is: The Global Elite. The Banksters. (But they also own everything else, including all the 'big' Corporations, and Governments, the media, and legal systems, etc). Referring back to what was said earlier, details of all of this have been exposed for at least 20 years by researching writers such as David Icke, Jordan Maxwell, William Cooper, and others. Others include Myron Fagan, Benjamin Friedman, and Jack Bernstein, going back as far as the 1960s. Even Charlie Chaplin could see 'something was very wrong'.

It is apparent to me that, while there has been much discussion on just who, exactly, the Global Elite are - naming names such as the Rothschilds, Rockefellers, Bronfmans, Webbs, Windsors, etc. - it seems it has yet to be explained just, exactly, what the Global Elite are, in terms of their obvious 'lack of humanity'. And what, and why, that is.

David Icke has referred to them as: *"Having no empathy"*. Which is true. They would not have created these Grand Deceptions if they had been 'nice people to do business with'.

Now, you'll probably resent knowing this, but you exist in a prison-without-bars. A prison that has been carefully constructed, over centuries, by those 'not very nice people to do business with'.

Unlike a real prison - where you see the bars - you'll firmly believe you are - basically - free. But, unfortunately, you are not. As each day goes by, your freedoms - many of which are essential for a decent and reasonable life - are being taken away from you by very subtle stealth.

And this has been going on for a very long time.

Hopefully, when you have read to the end of this book, you'll understand the prison, and will be able to see the bars, and be in the position of breaking out of them, using the enormous power you possess. Power you do not realise you actually have.

In his book *1984* George Orwell said: *"He who controls the present, controls the past. He who controls the past, controls the future"*.

To understand today, one must understand a certain amount of history. To understand the possibilities for future, one must understand today.

George Orwell also said: *"Omission is the biggest form of a lie"*. (One could, in point of fact, quote Orwell almost constantly. For the very simple reason that, in the 1940s, he actually gave us an amazing number of clues, through that book and his other masterpiece, *Animal Farm*)

'The past' means 'history'. How far back in history do we need to go?

Well, in point of fact you can go back as far as you wish. For the very simple reason that 'human nature' has always been with us. And the lessons we must learn derive from what happens when human nature is up against a 'less-than-human nature'.

What do I mean by that? I'll simply quote ONE, verifiable, medical/genetic statistic: ***"One in every 25 people are born psychopathic"***. That's a quote from the studious works of Psychologist Andrew M. Lobaczewski. See his book *Political Ponerology: A Science on the Nature of Evil Adjusted for Political Purposes (1998).*

Since there are 4 x 25s in every hundred, this means 4 people in every hundred, or 4% of the total population are psychopathic. According to my arithmetic, and taking the population of the United Kingdom as 60 million people, that means there are 2,400,000 psychopaths out there.

Do you think it might be a good idea to know this?

Does that mean 2.4 million 'axe murderers'? Well no, not exactly, as you will see, but it does mean that there is **the potential for** 2.4 million 'axe murderers'. Psychopaths-in-society tend to be much more subtle. (And get a heck of a lot further than axe murderers, as we will see).

It all comes down to what a psychopath actually is. Put simply it is a person who has no conscience. No compassion toward others. No empathy towards others. Unable to feel guilt, or shame.

How does this occur? It occurs because of the lack of a gene in such a person's DNA. The gene that creates 'feelings towards others'.

But a psychopath retains 'feelings towards themselves'. Although they don't feel guilt for any action they may take, they do feel 'fear'. And they know what would happen to them if they get caught. So they are afraid of getting caught. 'Fear of getting caught' is, in fact, **the only thing** that actually keeps them in check.

So, if the possibility of 'getting caught' can be eliminated, then the psycho has free rein. And that, fundamentally, is what has happened.

How has the possibility of getting caught been eliminated? Money and blackmail. If you have enough money, you can do anything. You can buy people off. You can arrange circumstances that create the possibilities for blackmail. You can arrange for 'character assassination' in the media (because you own the media!). You can arrange for actual assassinations. With sufficient money behind you, you can do anything.

Back in the 18th century, Amshel Rothschild said: *"Give me control of a nation's money supply, and I care not who makes the laws"*. Yes, the thing about these psychos is they catch on a lot quicker than most of us. Most people find the idea of a psycho hard to grasp at first sight. So it might be an idea to think about it in a little depth.

A baby is born. The baby looks like all others i.e. Winston Churchill. The baby learns to crawl, talk a bit, and to toddle. There is very little to distinguish this small person from any other.

It is only when this person becomes what we would call 'a child' that any symptoms might be detectable. And only then if we knew what we were looking for, and that is far from easy (in fact may not be possible), because all children can be naughty.

Picture a school playground. A child falls, or is knocked, over. Other children rush up, and say: *"Are you all right?"* or: *"Can I help you up?"*, and so on.

The psychopathic child sees this, and thinks: *"I don't know why they do that. They aren't hurt. Why should they care? I'm not hurt. I don't care"*. But, on the other hand, not to be seen as the odd one out, the psychopathic child learns to do the same. Not because they care, but just because they don't want to be seen as odd.

In short, a psycho learns 'how to emulate a conscience' - by observing the reactions of others.

During teenage years, as knowledge accumulates, and as situations come and go, the psycho could well be tempted to say (to themselves): *"You know, most people are stupid. They have a problem. They are forever looking out for others, when they should be looking out for themselves. Yes, they have a problem. I don't have that problem, I'm glad to say. I think they are inferior. I think I was born 'superior'. Perhaps I'm one of that 'master race' they told me about in school. The ones the Germans believed to exist, and fought WWII over"*.

And, gradually, it dawns on them: *"I can use this to my advantage! I know how to pretend, I've done that OK so far. So if I carry on pretending to care, no-one will realise that I can use my advantage, my superiority"*.

Consequent to all of this, they will generate - within themselves - a burning ambition to 'get to the top of the tree, by hook or by crook'. Letting nothing stand in their way. Before long they will consider it their 'destiny'. And they will justify this by saying to themselves: *"Hey, taking these people for a ride is good, because they leave themselves open to it. They actually ASK for it! They actually deserve it!"*

In business, when up for promotion, they will use every trick in the book - as long as they don't get caught - to get the job on offer. If other people's lives are ruined in the process ... so what?

And so on. Surely I've said enough to paint the overall picture?

Once in a position of 'power', it is then possible to promote psychos to staff the hierarchy below. And conjoin them, by various forms of blackmail, to provide protection from 'getting caught'. This could be the simple blackmail of: *"You rely on me for your job, never forget that"*. (That's very simple, but very powerful, blackmail ... is it not?).

Is it possible that such phrases as: *"It's dog eat dog out there"* or: *"There's no sentiment in business"* and: *"If I didn't do it, someone else would"* (and so on) could come straight out of the mouths of such people? Is it possible that such people could send thousands to fight, kill, maim, bomb innocent men, women, children and babies - in some foreign country - and they, themselves, still get a good night's sleep? No shame. No guilt. No responsibility for their actions. 'Justified' by their 'ability to take the hard decisions'?

Even to be caught endlessly lying, and yet still smile and carry on regardless? No shame. No guilt. (No resignation).

Does anyone see a connection here, between what I've said and British Prime Ministers? And US Presidents? And French Presidents? And German Chancellors? And UN Secretary-Generals? And EU Commissioners? Russian Presidents? In point of fact the 'leaders' of every nation on Earth?

Or am I just plain old paranoid?

Here is a quote from a Psychologist who fully admits to never actually interviewing Tony B Liar, having just had the (unpleasant) experience of analysing him via the TV screen (this quote dates from about 2004, when I received it in an e-mail): *"I have worked with a lot of psychopaths, and the one thing about them that is consistent is that whatever they are doing, their eyes rarely change. There is just a coldness there. You know, when a healthy person smiles their eyes 'light up' or conversely 'blaze' with anger. In all the pictures and TV broadcasts I've seen of Tony B-Liar [sic.], his eyes are always fixed - even when he's smiling as in the 'pictures of the God' comment.*

When a person starts saying that he consulted God about starting a war that led to the killing of innocent people as well as our own young servicemen, it's a sure sign he is suffering from psychopathy. Unfortunately it's not considered treatable under the Mental Health Act! Blair must be locked up in a Special Hospital forthwith. But some tribunal will probably let him out to kill again!"

Global Elite/Psychopaths

Note what was said by the Psychologist. 'Psychopathy' is the one major mental state for which the rest of society cannot be protected under the Mental Health Act.

Why did Tony B Liar make it so easy to collect your DNA at every possible opportunity? It goes back to the DNA, remember? DNA analysis can detect whether you are a psycho like Tony, or not.

DNA has nothing whatsoever to do with catching criminals, and Tony knew there are no terrorists to speak of - apart from himself and his gang of psychos. Your DNA is in your hair. Pick a stray hair from someone's jacket - in a restaurant - and you have something that can be left at a crime scene for the police to find.

How can that situation possibly work?

It can't.

Now let's summarise. Psychopaths have been around since the dawn of time. Their 'condition' gives themselves a driving ambition, to 'get to the top by hook or by crook'. But what's the point of getting to the top? There is only one point: **To dominate**. There is no point in having 'power' over others unless it is wielded, which provides the fuel for massive ego-massaging.

Quite why one should feel the driving desire to control others is something I don't, personally, understand. I don't understand the logic and rationale of their mindset. I don't see the point of their mindset. I don't see any ultimate point. I don't see how it can ever have any ultimate point. But I fully understand that they have that mindset.

Personally speaking, I think you should do your thing, and I do my thing, and we just all get along amicably - without me dominating you, or you dominating me. I can see that idea stretching into infinity without introducing rancour - rancour that would eventually generate revolution and bloodshed.

Consequently the psychopathic mindset is utterly myopic, in my humble opinion. But that has never stopped them from being clever. Fiendishly clever, in point of fact. And that did not stop them from playing a very, very, long term game. A game that the initiating psychos never expected to see the results of, but they thought their descendents would.

This attitude is the source of the 'Divine Right of Kings'. Which translates as: *"We are superior because we are uninhibited. We can make uninhibited, dispassionate, decisions with your life and limb".*

(Back in olden times of course the King also risked his own life and limb. But that all goes away as soon as a woman takes the throne i.e. Queen Elizabeth I, or Queens Anne, Victoria, Elizabeth II. And nowadays the Monarch only 'risks their children'. But that's only to some extent. By pulling strings, the 'risks' are minimised to almost nothing)

But, remember, it's all in the DNA. The 'compassion gene' could return, to the bloodline, if marriages are not very carefully arranged. Now do you understand why these bloodlines are kept 'pure'? It is to ensure that this pesky gene doesn't return so as to interfere with the 'Divine Right of Kings'.

We know what happens if that pesky gene returns. If someone from a psychopathic family, but in possession of a 'better nature', makes it to 'the top', then they are assassinated (JFK). And so is their brother (RFK). And their son (JFK Jr.). And so that pesky gene is eliminated.

This also happens if a non-psychopathic Pope attains that position. After 33 days, they are poisoned. Got to keep that pesky gene under control!

So that's what we are dealing with. Does it all make a lot more sense now? Does it explain why demonstrations, letter-writing campaigns, petitions and so forth - and elections - make not the slightest difference? Because all of these are appealing to the 'better nature' of creatures that do not possess a 'better nature'!

As you will see, if you read on, your only defence is to know your enemy, and put your foot down. Using the immense power you possess. Power you do not realise you have. The power to make decisions based on Common Sense, and to put those decisions into effect.

Chapter 6: Promises & Contracts

If Human A makes a promise to Human B, is Human C bound to honour that promise? We know this sort of thing happens, certainly within a family. Mum promises next-door neighbour that her son will come round tomorrow and fix the leaking guttering.

Meanwhile her son has arranged something for himself for tomorrow.

Get the picture? *"Oh ... Mum! I promised Steffie I would take her out tomorrow! Shit! You always do this to me!"*

It doesn't work, does it? No ... you can't go around making other people's promises. You can only make your own promises.

Common Sense.

So, what right does any Government have - to make promises on your behalf?

Well ... none really.

But there are exceptions. And I'll explain an obvious one by example. (Please do not accuse me of chauvinism. I write this example in the simplest way, so as to make the situation clear. You can substitute sexes as much as you wish. The result, the analogy, is precisely the same)

A secretary will run an Appointments Book for her boss. She will know his business inside and out, and will take calls on his behalf. And, when clients call, she will make appointments for him, and he will fulfill those appointments. Because he trusts her, and she trusts him.

The essence of this equitable situation is that little word 'trust'.

And, more importantly, this entire arrangement exists because both the secretary and the boss have 'consented' to it in the first place. He offered her the job, and she consented to accept it.

'Consent' and 'trust' are essential for a situation where one can make promises on behalf of someone else. 'Consent' and 'trust' are essential for equitable arrangements.

Otherwise it is not possible to make promises on behalf of someone else.

Common Sense?

If you don't trust your Government, then it has no right to make promises on your behalf.

Common Sense?

If the Government makes treaties with the European Union, then the Government is making promises with the European Union.

Not you. You are making no promises. And you cannot be held responsible and lawfully bound by any promises the Government may make. Only the Government is bound by the promises it makes.

Unless you consent to it, no-one has the right to make promises on your behalf. No-one (unless you consent!)

You really need to understand this. It's just plain Common Sense.

Don't moan you never got a Referendum. You always have a Referendum! It's called Lawful Rebellion, as we will see. (And you can do 90% of it from the comfort of your armchair).

But we will come to that. Let's keep on track, and put promises into context.

A Contract is: *"A promise the Law will enforce"*. That's the basic definition. But you may notice that is singular. Which refers, therefore to a singular Contract. There are such things but, for our purposes, they are not worth dwelling upon.

For our purposes, the Contracts that are important are those between two Parties - generally you and someone, or something, else.

Therefore I will explain the Contract as: *"A pair of interdependent mutually exchanged promises the Law will enforce"*, being the basic definition to examine.

For a Contract to be enforceable in Law, it must fulfill certain commonsense criteria. There are four of them, and they are designed to make sure the promises are sufficiently explicit, such that neither Party can later claim: *"I wasn't told about that bit!"*

These components are:

1. **Full Disclosure**: Which means that each Party writes down exactly what their promise comprises, and all the relevant circumstances, so as to put it into the context they consider applicable. If one has any sense, any necessary 'get outs' should be included within the Full Disclosure.

2. **Equal Considerations**: A Contractual Consideration is an 'item of value'. It may be money, or it may be an item. Both Parties must consider the exchange to be equal in value.

(As we have already seen, 'money' is an illusion, and is nothing more than an empty, meaningless IOU. Consequently most Contracts can be shown to fail in this respect, if one has the will to do that. This is explained later. One argument, when receiving a demand for money is: *'What do you want me to pay you with? Meaningless, empty-promise, worthless Debt Notes? Or do you want something of value, in which case you need to ask for it'*).

Obviously for Considerations to be equal they cannot change, once agreed. Thus any Contract employing variable Interest Rates is null & void in Law. Accepting the validity of variable Considerations, and not standing up against them, is precisely how so many people embroil themselves in debt.

And, in any case – as we will see when we re-consider 'money' in the Chapter on *Mass Mind Control & Enslavement*, the funds to create 'Interest' forms no part of our Monetary Belief System. Or, to put this another way, 'Interest' is nowhere created, and consequently it is impossible to pay off all loans, and impossible for everyone to stay out of bankruptcy. Those who stay out of bankruptcy are doing so purely on the backs of those who enter bankruptcy – purely because they were simply the first to grab whatever was available. (Whether they realise this or not).

Oh! And did I mention the real dooley? A lawful Contractual Consideration must come **entirely from each Party's own resources**. This is where just about every 'supposed' Contract breaks down. For example, a loan or mortgage will **not** have come from whoever issued it. It will have come from thin air. This can be shown to be the case by demanding the full accounting, showing where the 'money' actually came from. The answer will be: *"Nowhere but keystrokes. The bank just typed a few numbers into one of their computers"*.

The 'Banking', 'Loaning' and 'Credit' Systems are totally illegitimate, in reality. They depend entirely for their legitimacy on Governments saying: *"This is OK for banks to do, but for anyone else it is fraud/deception/counterfeiting"*.

And the reasons for this attitude are known, in the vernacular, as 'kick-backs'. *"You didn't give a kick-back? Oh, then creating 'money' out of thin air is fraud! Counterfeiting! You did give a kick-back? You gave us the ability to just print 'money'? Oh, creating 'money' out of nothing is perfectly legal, then!"* That's the way it works. But 'demanding the full accounting' does tend to cause just a few little problems with that mechanism. Simply because the full accounting doesn't, actually, exist.

3. **Lawful Terms and Conditions**: Which, fundamentally, means that there should be no mischief in the proposed agreements.

4. **Mutual Intent**: Which means 'some manifestation that each Party intended to Contract'. This could be hand-written signature 'marks', or can be 'conduct'. In other words if at least one of the Parties starts to do

what was promised. This is sometimes expressed as 'performance' - or, at least, 'the start of performance'.

You have, probably without realising it, entered into many Contracts in your life. And, as we shall see, most of them are null and void in Law, because (even allowing for the small print) they fail on at least one of the components 1, 2, 3 or 4.

The most important thing to realise is that no 'small print' can override the fundamental aspects a Contract must fulfill in order to be lawful, and therefore enforceable. 'Invalid small print' does not actually nullify a Contract, but its provisions are irrelevant because they are unenforceable in Law. Therefore any Contract that **relies upon** unenforceable small print (for example variable Interest Rates) is – to all intents and purposes – null & void. **But you have to say so. A Court will not say it for you.**

And this provides the necessary 'get-outs'. Ultimately, at any rate. However, as we shall see, you have many more get-outs before resorting to nullifying Contractual Obligations. Nevertheless it is always a good idea to keep these points in mind, and not to forget them. For the simple reason that you will gain confidence by knowing that - at the end of the day - you can actually win any-which-way.

Previously I referred to your immense power. Part of your power is this knowledge. And the fact that those you deal with (I call them the Organic Robots) have absolutely no understanding of this at all. They just operate 'by rote'. And this includes the vast majority of the so-called 'Legal Profession'. This enables you to run rings around them.

There are a number of other points. One of the main ones being that: *"Adding something to the Contract once it has started is not allowed"*. There are many instances where this happens. A prime example of this is 'upping the Interest Rate'. No! No! No! That's a breach of Contract, matey! You can't adjust the Considerations once they have been agreed! Once agreed, they are fixed. And it's no good writing them into the Contract in the first place. If you write unlawful Conditions into a Contract, then those provisions are not enforceable. **Only the lawful Conditions are enforceable in Law**.

But you have to say so. Otherwise they will walk all over you.

But there are some very subtle ones as well. If, when you buy something, the Terms & Conditions are inside the box, then they are null & void. The Contract started when you handed over the money to purchase the item. At that point, if the Terms & Conditions were not made absolutely clear to you (before you handed over the money), then appraising you of them, in a booklet, inside the box, is: *"Too bloody late, mate!"*.

This is all absolute Common Sense, if you think about it. Anything else defines a moving target, a rug that can be pulled away from under you. Human Beings cannot interact reasonably, sensibly and peacefully on that sort of basis, can they? No-one would know where they stood, would they?

And, that's the point. That's precisely why you never know where you really stand. Because you don't know the basics of how Contracts work. You assume you must do what you are told. And you do. And that results in not knowing where you stand.

If your Common Sense tells you something is wrong, then it is telling you the truth. Something ***is*** wrong (***very*** wrong!). Hopefully (as I keep saying) by the time you have read this book, you will know exactly what to do about it.

Chapter 7: Honour, Dishonour & Noticing

It all comes down to this. In the Chapter on *Taking* I explained that there is no dishonour in doing that in order to survive in reasonable comfort. Dishonour comes from just being thoroughly greedy.

On a day-to-day basis there is more than that, if you decide you want to do something, as most people are doing all the time.

If you feel that what you want to do affects no-one else at all, then you just do it. I feel like making a cup of tea. So I just do it. I don't ask anyone else.

But there are many things that could easily affect someone else. And, I would guess, we would all think it reasonable to be a little bit more cautious in those circumstances. After all, we don't want repercussions, do we?

So how do you go about that? How do you do something honourably?

The answer is to give anyone who may be affected some notice. In other words you send them a Notice. (You 'Notice' them).

Well, that's OK so far. You can write down what you plan to do, explaining it in a letter. And send it to whomsoever you feel may be affected by your plan.

And you tell them, in your letter: *"Please let me know if you object, giving me your reasons. Thank you very much"*.

And then, if you receive objections, you negotiate amicably, to arrive at an arrangement that is acceptable to all.

Well, that's easy enough, isn't it?

No? It's not that easy? What happens if - as normal - they ignore you? So you don't receive any objections, and you just go ahead, and **then** they object!?

Ahh! Problem! Well, this can be taken care of, with honour.

What you do, within the Notice you send, is to explain that you are going to assume a reasonable time to receive objections. Quite often this is 14 days, but it can be longer or shorter depending on how you feel. You can choose the period, of course, but it is only honourable to be reasonable.

Honour, Dishonour & Noticing

You say that, if you don't hear back after the time period has elapsed, then you have the Right to assume they don't object.

As a Human Being you **do** have that Natural, Inalienable, Right.

If you do not get any response to your Notice, within the time period you have stated, then you have the right to assume 'acquiescence'. In other words 'tacit consent' to your plan.

(It is always a good idea to send your Notice by Registered Post, although the so-called 'Legal Profession', and most Officious Bodies, employ a rule that says: *"A letter sent with a First Class stamp affixed is good enough for service to be assumed"*. Quite how they think they can get away with that is totally beyond me. But then, as I said in the Chapter discussing *Legalese*, the 'legal world' is an illusory world, devoid of any rationality at all).

You can also send a reminder, giving a time period extension. This would be looked upon more favourably as more honourable, however (in my experience) a response is still unlikely, if you didn't get one from the original Notice.

This is generally because most people don't understand what 'being honourable' is all about. The assumption is that, if they need to object, they can do that if you go ahead.

Wrong! Once you have Noticed them lawfully, they no longer have any power of objection. Of course, you need to know that yourself, and to stand on it. You may receive very intimidating letters from someone's Solicitors. You simply need to write the appropriate reply.

The reply should point out that you have acted honourably, and supplied due Notice. (You would send them a copy of your original Notice). You point out that you allowed for objections, and received none in the set timescale. You then point out that you have obtained, by these **honourable** actions on your part: *"Permanent and irrevocable lawful estoppel by acquiescence"*.

That shuts them up. (Well, it would shut most people up, wouldn't it? Well, I think it would make anyone blink quite a few times, and take a few sharp intakes of breath, at the very least).

Bear in mind a Solicitor will know what 'estoppel' means. He or she won't know very much, but they will know that. It is a lawful 'gag'. An injunction if you will. One that you can create for yourself. It is designed to say: *"Look! Enough is enough! This cannot go on forever. There has to be a cut-off, and this is it! The to-ing and fro-ing stops here. The buck stops here. No more! Cease! Desist! I have acted honourably, and you/your Client have not. The Law says so. So you can sod off, and you know you can"*.

Yes, it shuts them up all right. And. They. Do. Not. Like. It. Up 'em!

As a sting in the tail, you can Notice the Solicitor that further correspondence with him or her in the matter will be charged at £500 (or £500,000 if you like … anything you like … you set the rate) per letter. They do that, and so can you. You can do this to anyone. (Debt Collecting Agencies are good ones to be on the receiving end of this sort of thing, as we will see later)

It's all just Common Sense; So don't be surprised if 'the line suddenly goes dead'.

Long Live Lawful Rebellion!

Chapter 8: Societies & Statutes

I referred to Statutes in the Chapter on *Legalese.* Now I come to explain them in more detail. We are told we live in a society. I stress: *"We are told that"*. And no-one argues because they assume they know what it means.

But - just a minute! Hold on there! There are things called 'societies' that you don't live in. The Law Society, for example. Do you live in The Law Society? I doubt it. Really 'live in' should be: *"Am an accredited Member of"*, because Societies have Memberships, don't they?

Well, yes they do. Societies are actually defined in a number of ways. Firstly a Name, secondly a Mission Statement, thirdly a Set of Society Rules, and lastly a Membership.

Here's Chambers Online (wrong again!):

society noun (societies) 1 humankind as a whole, or a part of it such as one nation, considered as a single community. 2 a division of humankind with common characteristics, eg of nationality, race or religion. 3 an organized group or association, meeting to share a common interest or activity o I'm a member of the gliding society. 4 a the rich and fashionable section of the upper class; b the social scene of this class section; c as adj o a society wedding. 5 formal company o He prefers the society of women. 6 ecol a small plant community within a larger group.

(1) & (2) conflict, logically, with (3), (4), (5) and (6). That's why it's wrong.

(3) is basically what 'a Society' is, in fact.

The essential point being the Membership aspect.

Societies need to be joined. Members have to apply for Membership, and be accepted as Members.

Get the idea? When did you apply for Membership of the Human Species?

No, the Human Species is not 'a Society'. It is 'Mankind', or 'the Human Species' or 'Homo Sapiens' ... make your choice ... but 'a Society' it is not!

And don't let them fool you that it is. Even if they manage to do that, don't forget the other thing about Societies. You apply for Membership because you feel the Mission Statement is something you support. And you want to help.

But - if the Society starts off down a road you don't agree with - **you can always resign!**

If the Human Species is 'a Society' … how can you resign? Death is the only obvious resignation, but I think that's just a little drastic, myself.

Personally I go for: *"'Scuse me! I was never asked whether or not I wanted to join. I don't, therefore, consider I have joined … whatever anyone else may think. I consider I have been thoroughly deceived, throughout my entire life. I don't need to submit my resignation, because I was only joined as a Member on someone else's assumption in the first place. And that doesn't count, as far as I'm concerned".*

Now, a Statute is defined as 'A legislated rule of a Society'.

So how can a Statute apply to you, if you are not a Member of the Society?

Answer: It can't. What is happening here resonates back with the business of 'someone making promises on someone else's behalf'.

No can do. No way, Jose!

You might be finding this all a bit tricky, but hold on tight. An explanation is looming on the horizon. In fact it is getting closer as you read. It might, just might, make you stand up, rush to the door, open it, run into the middle of the road, and shout (at the top of your voice): *"Halley-bloody-loo-yah!"*

This is the missing piece of the jigsaw: The United Kingdom is a Society. The united States of America are also Societies. And so are most of (what we call) 'countries' on this planet.

We call them Countries. Because we never knew any different. However a very long time ago, the Countries, the Nations, were re-organised into CORPORATIONS, for the convenience of the Global Elite.

They are listed on Dun & Bradstreet. On said website you can obtain Credit Reports on them. Everything is CORPORATONS. The Ministry of Justice is a CORPORATION, HM Treasury is a CORPORATION. The Police Force is a CORPORATION. (The UK Police have no more authority than Securicor. Or Group4).

When the Police make an arrest, it has the authority of a Citizen's Arrest. And nothing more. A Citizen's Arrest backed up with 'numbers', 'muscle' and 'technology'. But a Citizen's Arrest, all the same. We pay them to protect us, using 'numbers', 'muscle' and 'technology', to make

Citizen's Arrests. That's their job. That's what they swear to do by their Oaths of Service. That's all one set of Human Beings could do … to other Human Beings. If 'all are equal' (under the Law), what else could there ever be?

Even the British Labour Party is the Trading Name of a CORPORATION called 'ALASTAIR DARLING, MP' (at the time of writing).

Also note that there is another CORPORATION, called 'MEMBERS OF PARLIAMENT', and yet another called 'HM QUEEN ELIZABETH II'

Getting the idea?

So, what does this mean? It means that Statutes passed by a CORPORATION called 'MEMBERS OF PARLIAMENT' are the 'legislated rules' of the CORPORATION known as 'THE UNITED KINGDOM CORPORATION'.

They are **the Company Policy** of the CORPORATION known as 'THE UNITED KINGDOM CORPORATION'.

And, if you don't work for that CORPORATION - if you are not a Member (i.e. employee) of that CORPORATION, **then the 'legislated rules' don't apply to you**.

I'll repeat this, in order to drive it home. Statutes do not apply to you, unless you are a Member of a CORPORATION called 'THE UNITED KINGDOM CORPORATION'. (These legislated rules being created by the sub-CORPORATION, designed for that purpose, called 'MEMBERS OF PARLIAMENT'.

Are you a Member of THE UNITED KINGDOM CORPORATION?

When did you apply? Was your Membership request accepted?

The answer is: Your parents applied when you were born. Because they Registered your birth. And, in doing so, a Legal Fiction Person was automatically created for you as a Member of THE UNITED KINGDOM CORPORATION. *Legal Fiction Persons* are described in their own Chapter.

However, it is very doubtful that your parents realised what they were actually doing at the time, and thought they were under an obligation to do what they did. In the same way that you may very well have done the same thing in the case of your own children.

No recriminations, therefore.

And no recriminations really necessary - for the simple reason that, Common Sense must tell you, Full Disclosure never occurred at the time - otherwise no Registrations would (I think it can be reasonably assumed) ever have occurred. No-one in their right mind, appraised of all the facts, would willingly hand over their newborn to become an employee of a massive conglomerate CORPORATION.

Any assumed Contract, between your parents and that CORPORATION is null & void (in Law), due to lack of Full Disclosure, lack of Equal Consideration, and lack of Intent to Contract.

Bingo! You are free, because you say you are free!

All you have to do is to remember: The Organic Robots haven't a clue about all this, and they have loads of 'numbers' and loads of 'muscle'. They have brawn, but no brains.

On the other hand you will tend to be dealing with only one or two at any given time. Consequently the best thing to do is to tie them up in knots ... before they get the chance to reach for the 'muscle'.

Chapter 9: Common Law, The Law-of-the-Land

Now we are cooking on gas! This is where it all starts and it all ends. What is Common Law? Well it really doesn't matter what any dictionary says. However let's have a quick look at what Osborn's Concise Law Dictionary (10th Edition) says:

"That part of the law of England formulated, developed and administered by the old common law courts based originally on the common customs of the country, and unwritten. It is opposed to equity (the body of rules administered by the Court of Chancery); to statute law (the law laid down in Acts of Parliament); to special law (the law administered in special courts such as ecclesiastical law and the law merchant); and to the civil law (the law of Rome). It is "the commonsense of the community, crystalised and formulated by our forefathers". It is not local law, nor the result of legislation".

That's as good a definition as any. Because, in short, Common Law 'is'.

It just 'is'.

It is there.

No ducking. No diving. No weaving. No way out. Applicable to all. From the highest to the most lowly. That's what the definition says.

But then, who wants a way out? Common Law (commonsense) says the way to live peacefully is to:

1) **Not breach the peace;**
2) **Cause no-one else any harm;**
3) **Cause no-one else any loss;**
4) **Not use mischief in your promises and agreements.**

Personally speaking, I have no problem whatsoever with that. In point of fact I fully welcome it as, I submit, so would any sane, reasonable, and responsible Human Being.

Common Law is **the Law-of-the-Land**. It is the Law that has come about by means of the customs & traditions of Land-Dwellers.

And, the point is, Parliament has absolutely no say in Common Law. It is there, and they cannot touch it. In point of fact, Parliament (and Congress) **is actually bound by it**. Just like everyone else. (Not that they realise that, of course. One of the biggest 'upsets' on the horizon will come when enough people realise this, and bring them to book for their gross negligence).

The only 'law' that Parliament can create (since the Law-of-the-Land has already been created) is the Law-of-Waters. Hence Statutes are the Law-of-Waters. And Statutes need your consent, before they can be applied to you, if you are located on dry land.

In this case you need to become a Member of the UNITED KINGDOM CORPORATION, and for Legalese Fictional purposes actually be prepared to be considered as 'a ship on the ocean'. There is more detail about this in the Chapter on the *Law-of-Waters*, which has its own Chapter in this book.

Common Law = Common Sense. It has been developed over centuries, within Case Law, to have - by now - squeezed just about every drop of justice out of just about every conceivable, fundamental, situation - where Human Beings are involved and interact.

Advances in technology are irrelevant. Common Law rests entirely on 'the Human Condition'. Has one individual behaved honourably, or not? That sort of thing.

It is based fair and square on the 'customs & traditions' from the ancient past. Customs & traditions that were evolved, in a codified manner, so as to create peaceful co-existence all round.

Just look at the principles, above. What else is necessary? Answer: Nothing. Stick to those principles, and nothing else is necessary.

It has been said: *"Look into your heart. Use your Common Sense to know what is right and what is wrong. If what you want to do is fair, and just, then you can do it"*.

No amount of Common Law deviates from these principles.

Only legislated Statutes aka Company Policy of THE UNITED KINGDOM CORPORATION or THE UNITED STATES OF AMERICA CORPORATION (etc.), deviate from these principles.

Any deviation is null and void.

But you have to say so. You have to understand what is happening, and to firmly, and politely, stand your ground. The *Examples*, in the Appendices of this book, indicate ways of doing that.

I wrote about *Notices* (there is a Chapter on them). And how you can 'put someone on Notice about your intentions'. And how you can create an estoppel. What you are actually doing is **making** Common Law.

If you take a Solemn Oath, you are **making** Common Law. If you create an Affidavit, you are **making** Common Law. Because, in either case, you are stating Your Truth - as you see it. And you have the right to state Your Truth, as you see it.

That's why Common Law is so ephemeral. It's everywhere. Provided you do not deviate from the principles - provided that you act with honour - you are making Your Own Common Law!

You are saying: *"This is My Custom. This is My Tradition. And I will stick to these peaceful principles".*

Common Sense … yet again!

After all, what **is** the Law, anyway? How does it come about?

Consensus facit legem. **Consent makes the Law.**

The consent of the overwhelming majority, whose one primary desire is to live their lives in peace. In peaceful co-existence with everyone else.

Free to do whatever it is they choose to do, provided they do not adversely affect anyone else. Free to travel at will. Free to express opinions. Free to exchange. And so on. Freedom from imposed fictions & illusions. Freedom from tyranny. Freedom from the domination of the many by the few.

And those Common Sense desires were codified in Common Law, as a protection of it.

And this was done many centuries ago. It formed the basis of the Magna Carta, the US Constitution, the French Constitution, and so on. It actually forms the basis of every Constitution ever written. (Any Constitution worth its salt, that is). There is an Appendix dedicated to the *Magna Carta 1215*, and it is well worth reading.

So the ideas are not new. In point of fact the ideas are so old, we seem to have forgotten them. It is my sincere hope that this book serves as an appropriate reminder.

Do you consent to live in peace? I hope you do, otherwise this book is not for you.

Do you consent to pay for the use of your own property, once purchased? Your dwelling (Council Tax), your conveyance (Road Tax), your entertainment (TV Licence)? Bearing in mind, of course, that none of these impositions on your freedom actually fund whatever it is they purport. That, in point of fact, they fund just about everything else besides. Do you consent to aiding & abetting War Crimes?

You don't? Well, in that case there is no Law by Consent.

Is there?

Chapter 10: Notices, Invitations & Summonses

I group these together because they are all, essentially, the same thing. They are 'offers to Contract'. You see, a Summons (for example) is not something that should make your knees go to jelly. A Summons is just a Notice that should be read as: *"An invitation to go to a place of business, at a certain time, and on a certain date, in order to be made an offer for a service"*.

The service in question being the one of 'adjudication'. 'Arbitration' if you want to call it that. And you are perfectly entitled to write back: *"No thanks. Your services are not required"*.

Whhaaaaat!?! When you receive a Summons there will be accompanying paperwork. You will be offered the chance to plead guilty or not guilty, to the charge made against you. Actually, as you will see in the appropriate Chapter, the charge is not levelled at you - it is levelled at your *Legal Fiction Person.*

Nevertheless, by pleading guilty or not guilty, you are accepting the service of arbitration that is on offer, and in doing so you are admitting responsibility for your Legal Fiction Person.

However if, instead of pleading, you make it quite clear that you are not the Legal Fiction Person, but are actually a living, breathing, Human Being with a soul, and live in the real world of Common Law, then you are perfectly entitled to write back : *"No thanks. Your services are not required. Good day"*, as I explained, above.

You do this in the form of a Notice. Their Summons to you was a Notice. You respond with a Notice of your own. And, in the same way they would have put a time-limit of the Summons (it may very well be the Court Date), then you can put a time-limit, for the Court's response, on your Notice back to them.

You would head your Notice something like: **NOTICE OF NON-ACCEPTANCE OF OFFERED SERVICES AND REQUEST FOR CLARIFICATION**.

You would then write a letter explaining that you are a Human Being, and would they please clarify the situation, because the Summons was addressed to a Legal Fiction Person, which you cannot accept as such, but you wish to know how you, as a Human Being, have dishonoured any **lawful** obligation on your part.

Notices, Invitations & Summonses

Remember: The charge against your Legal Fiction Person will be based in the fictional and illusory world of Legalese & Statutes. You need them to show which Common Law Principle your Human Self has breached.

They will not be able to do this. The Court will probably ignore your Notice, which will place **itself** (they, themselves) in dishonour. It may be necessary to actually go to the Court, at the date & time of the Hearing, and to point out their own dishonour.

Fundamentally by claiming Common Law jurisdiction. All is explained in the Chapter on *Courts & Proceedings*. It is likely to be a very short Hearing. Probably about a minute or so, before you walk out with an enormous smile on your face. **If you do it right**. And that means understanding **everything** in this book.

Chapter 11: Legal Fiction Person

The Legal Fiction Person is mentioned frequently in this book. It is one of the basic irrationalities of Legalese. But Legalese exists. Anything to do with the Courts or the Police, **in relation to Statutes**, is bound up in Legalese.

On a practical note it is no good just telling a Solicitor, or a Magistrate or a Judge, or a Policeman that they live in a fictional world of illusion.

They do. But their world is so ingrained they will not believe you. They even find it impossible to recognise their own double-think. Of course, one of the most important things about double-think is that you can only do it as long as you can't recognise you are doing it. (In that sense it is self-fulfilling, aka self-supporting)

What you need to do is to know the score, and know how to duck.

One of the primary components of knowing the score is to know when something that drops on your doormat is addressing you, or your Legal Fiction Person. If it is addressed to you, Your Human Self, then you'll need to deal with it, in order to avoid dishonour.

If it is addressed to your Legal Fiction Person, then there are other ways of dealing. Primarily to place a Universe between Your Human Self and your Legal Fiction Person. (Sometimes called: *"Tin-plating your own backside"*).

So, there are three things you need to know:

1. What is a Legal Fiction Person, anyway?

2. How do you recognise your Legal Fiction Person being addressed?

3. How do you tin-plate the backside of Your Human Self?

First of all, a Legal Fiction Person is often referred to as a STRAWMAN. The reason for this is that the letter addressed to the STRAWMAN is, actually, clutching at a straw. If you respond as people normally do - because they do not recognise the situation - then the grasp at the straw will succeed.

If you respond as explained in this book, the clutch at the straw will come away empty-handed.

This is possibly one of the hardest concepts to grasp. The use of the word 'person', in Legalese, is very subtle and very clever. Simply because most Human Beings will consider themselves to be 'a person'. And, of course, in Oxford English, they are.

The best analogy I have heard is that the word 'person' comes, originally, from the word 'persona'. And you need to consider what a 'persona' actually is.

It is your outward manifestation presented to the 5-sense world. It is what you present, as yourself, to the world at any given time. It is very much tied to your personality. (After all, the word 'person' is the stem of the word 'personality').

It can be thought of as a mask. Or an overcoat. One or more you can wear, when circumstances permit.

In wet weather your overcoat would need to be a rainproof.

In cold weather your overcoat would need to be one that keeps you warm, rather than just rainproof.

Do you get the idea?

In the circle of your family & friends your persona would generally be friendly and kindly.

In the presence of an enemy your persona would be hateful.

Your persona depends on the circumstances you are in, at any given time. However you, Your Self, are exactly the same flesh & blood & soul irrespective of the circumstances. You are always the same sovereign Human Being, with a living soul.

You are **not** your persona. You are **you**. You take on a persona (wear a persona) according to circumstances. You could also think of it as wearing different masks. (By the way, you are **not** your Name, either. See the Chapter on *Names*).

The clutch at the straw is attempting to make You, Your Self, The Human Being, wear the Legal Fictional Person 'overcoat' or 'mask'.

It is necessary to get you to wear this overcoat or mask because that means you accept your role or employment as a Member of THE UNITED KINGDOM CORPORATION, to whom the Company Policy applies. (To whom the Statutes apply).

As a free Human Being you can choose to wear this mask, or not. If you understand what is really happening, you would almost certainly **not** choose to do so. If you don't wear the Legal Fiction Person mask then you are not a Member of THE UNITED KINGDOM CORPORATION, and its rules don't apply to you. Its Company Policy has no force of law upon you. You can just walk away.

That's why you are perfectly entitled to say: *"No thanks. Your services are not required. Good day"*, as I explained in the Chapter on *Notices, Invitations & Summonses.*

So how do you recognise a letter addressed to your Legal Fiction Person?

Well, first of all, there is such a thing as a Legal Fiction Status. Or 'Title', such as '**Mr.**', '**Mrs.**', '**Miss**', '**Ms.**', and so on. These are fictional titles! They have no meaning at all! They might be considered to be a politeness, but - once you recognise what they actually do - they are a long, long, way from being polite.

They are a long way from being polite, because they create a Legal Fiction Person. A STRAWMAN. And when present as the first line of the address on a Demand or Summons, etc., they represent an attempt to fraudulently shake you down. To extract money from you, with menaces. And that's not what I call 'polite'.

This is the most common way of addressing a Legal Fiction Person. It is generally accompanied by writing all or a part of your name in CAPITALS.

Actually a 'Name' is a Legal Fiction as well. In order to be free, you do not have a Name. Instead 'you respond to what you are commonly called'. What 'you are commonly called' can be written by placing colon ("**:**") after your Given Names (all Given Names hyphenated together), and then writing your Family Name.

This book has been written by Veronica: Chapman (for short) … as commonly called … or Veronica: of the Chapman family (for long).

In practice, since this Lawful Rebellion is all so new to the world, and the Organic Robots have yet to come to terms with it, I do accept "Veronica Chapman" as addressing My Human Self.

In other words I do not stamp my foot at the missing colon. However I flatly reject '**Ms.**' or '**Miss**' prepended. That's Legal Fiction Statusville.

However perhaps I should point out that this system of writing 'what you are commonly called' - has no 'legal basis'. It is just a convention that has been adopted by those in Lawful Rebellion. Can we do that? Yes … of course we can! Why the hell not? The fact that it has no 'legal basis' is good, because it separates us from the illusory world of Legalese.

Chapter 12: Solicitors, Lawyers & Notaries

What is the **first** duty of your Legal Representative? To you, the Client? Gosh, no! Wrong! The first duty of a Legal Representative is to the Court. Then to the public. And then to you, the Client.

So, if the Court barks, your Legal Representative jumps!

What is your relationship to the Court if you are legally represented?

You are being **re-presented to the Court** (represented in Court) as an 'imbecilic child'. It doesn't matter what your actual age is, in years. As far as the Court is concerned you are a 'ward of the Court'. You are considered a 'child', and your Legal Representative is the 'adult' who is looking after you.

And you are expected to pay for the privilege of being viewed in this way.

Actually, it does all make sense. In the illusory world of Legalese. You are - to all intents and purposes - a non-comprehending creature (a child in essence), and you do need an 'adult' looking after you. An adult who understands Legalese, and therefore what is going on.

So, here is yet another reason for, firstly, representing Your Self, and secondly standing on Common Law - thus avoiding any contact with Legalese, and the 'legal' world. And remaining within the real world of Common Sense.

Very few, if any, Solicitors and/or Lawyers are prepared to defend you on Common Law principles. They will tell you it is: *"Baseless"*. That it has: *"No legal standing"*.

Of course it is perfectly true that it: *"Has no legal standing"*. Absolutely!

But the point is that: ***"It has LAWFUL standing"***, and that always trumps 'legal standing', so it is a zillion miles from 'baseless'.

The Court system does not like this. It hates what it calls Litigants-in-Person, because that upsets its apple cart. They. Do. Not. Like. It. Up 'em!

How is this derived? Well consider the sections from the Corpus Juris Secundum (C.J.S.) legal encyclopedia, volume 7, section 4, in Figures 1 through 4.

To what or whom is an attorney's first duty? See Figure 1.

What is the legal relationship between an attorney and his/her client? See Figure 2.

§ 4 ATTORNEY & CLIENT 7 C. J. S.

His first duty is to the courts and the public, not to the client,[15] and wherever the duties to his client conflict with those he owes as an officer of the court in the administration of justice, the former must yield to the latter.[16]

The office of attorney is indispensable to the administration of justice and is intimate and peculiar in its relation to, and vital to the well-being of, the court.[17] An attorney has a duty to aid the court in seeing that actions and proceedings in which he is engaged as counsel are conducted in a dignified and orderly manner, free from passion and personal animosities, and that all causes brought to an issue are tried and decided on their merits only;[18] to aid the court

Figure 1: The relationship between Legal Representative & Client

§§ 2-3 ATTORNEY & CLIENT 7 C. J. S.

and the term is synonymous with "attorney."[13] Therefore, anyone advertising himself as a lawyer holds himself out to be an attorney, an attorney at law, or counselor at law.[15]

If one appears before any court in the interest of another and moves the court to action with respect to any matter before it of a legal nature, such person appears as an "advocate", as that term is generally understood.[16] The phrase "as an advocate in a representative capacity," as used in the statute regulating the practice of law, implies a representation distinct from officer or other regular administrative corporate employee representation.[17]

In England and her colonies a "barrister" is a person entitled to practice as an advocate or counsel in the superior courts.[18] A "solicitor" is a person whose business it is to be employed in the care and management of suits depending in courts of chancery.[19] In the great majority of the states of the Union, where law and equity are both administered by the same court, it has naturally come about that the two offices of attorney at law and solicitor in chancery have practically been consolidated, although in the federal equity practice the term "solicitor" is in general use; but in some states the office of solicitor in chancery is a distinct and separate office from that of attorney at law.[20]

A client is one who applies to a lawyer or counselor for advice and direction in a question of law, or commits his cause to his management in prosecuting a claim or defending against a suit in a court of justice;[21] one who retains the attorney, is responsible to him for his fees, and to whom the attorney is responsible for the management of the suit;[22] one who communicates facts to an attorney expecting professional advice.[23] Clients are also called "wards of the court" in regard to their relationship with their attorneys.[24]

§ 3. Nature of Right to Practice

While it has been broadly stated that the right to practice law is not a natural or constitutional right, but is in the nature of a privilege or franchise, the practice of law is not a matter of grace but of right for one who is qualified by his learning and moral character.

Library References

Attorney and Client ⊜14.

The right to practice law is not a natural or constitutional right.[25] Nor is the right to practice

Figure 2: The relationship between You & the Court.

Wards of court. **Infants and persons of unsound mind placed by the court under the care of a guardian. Davis' Committee v. Loney, 290 Ky. 644, 162 S.W.2d 189, 190. Their rights must be guarded jealously. Montgomery v. Erie R. Co., C.C.A.N.J., 97 F.2d 289, 292.** ***See*** **Guardianship.**

Figure 3: A Ward of the Court.

In propria persona /in prówpriyə pərsównə/. In one's own proper person. It was formerly a rule in pleading that pleas to the jurisdiction of the court must be plead *in propria persona,* because if pleaded by attorney they admit the jurisdiction, as an attorney is an officer of the court, and he is presumed to plead after having obtained leave, which admits the jurisdiction. *See* Pro se.

Figure 4: A Litigant-in-Person.

What is a ward of the court? See Figure 3.

Do you need to challenge jurisdiction? Better see Figure 4, particularly the part that says: "... *because if pleaded by an attorney ...*". **It means you accept the jurisdiction of the Court**.

Chapter 13: Veronica's Very Cunning 2-Step Plan for Freedom

I already mentioned this in the Foreword, but I need to expand upon it. These steps are nothing more than Common Sense. And that is the same as Common Law. And most nations on this planet operate under Common Law as a fundamental basis, particularly those that - historically - were spawned from the British Isles (e.g. the united States of America and Commonwealth countries, left over from the days of the British Empire).

Step 1: You are free because **you say** you are free. Because no-one else will. You have to **think** free 24/7, **be** free 24/7 and **act** free 24/7.

If you don't do that, then you are faking it, and playing with fire, and are likely to get your fingers burned.

Step 2: You have to ensure everyone else recognises it, and treats you accordingly. This is the tricky bit. You have to be prepared to lead by example. You have to learn what freedom is - which means taking the full responsibility for your words and deeds, such that you peacefully co-exist with all other lifeforms as far as possible. You have to think - seriously - about what that means.

You have to learn that breaching the peace is a serious offence against all Common Sense, and (therefore) Common Law. That causing harm or loss to another is also against Common Sense and Common Law. That employing mischief in your daily business is likewise against Common Sense and Common Law. Anything that **deliberately** provokes or causes rancour is contrary to Common Sense and Common Law - and these, therefore, are not only basic crimes, but the only crimes.

Those are the basics and, once you understand them, everything else falls naturally into place.

In point of fact Common Sense is worldwide ... stemming from humanity itself. The exceptions are strongly religious States who suppress Common Sense with irrational dogma. It is hard to understand how those poor souls can ever be free, but one must, I suppose, never give up hope for them.

WWIII has been raging since the end of WWII. We were led to believe that WWIII would be the ultimate Nuclear War. Since we have been deceived in all other areas of our lives, it is no surprise to find that we were deceived in that respect as well. WWIII is an **Information** War. A war for the control of your Mind. And the applied Mind Control has been tremendously successful in that respect, to the point where it has become ingrained.

The Freedom Movement is the antithesis of Mind Control. The Freedom Movement says: *"Step out of being a Mind-Controlled Organic Robot, and start thinking for yourself. Look into your heart. Listen to it. All the answers are there"*. And that's all the Freedom Movement says. The rest is just left to your Common Sense.

However this does not mean to say you have to take everything on board all at the same time. There is plenty of room for edging your way into Lawful Rebellion. For example, you do not have to abandon your National Insurance Number until you can make it on your own. It would be stupid to do that. There is nothing to stop you using it less and less, until - one day - you can say: *"I don't need that any more"*.

You can claim the Rights via a ***Notice of Understanding and Intent and Claim of Right***, and I have included mine in an Appendix. This does not mean I have to immediately execute the Rights I claimed. I can leave them in abeyance for as long as I like. That's entirely my own choice. Just because one may possess a bicycle, doesn't mean one can't go to work in one's car. (Especially if it is raining).

You might find it more effective to simply introduce these ideas to as many friends as possible (rather than anything else), by starting a local group of like-minded individuals. Then you may very well find that you can arrange things in a way that is equitable to all. Apart from spreading the word, this also helps to keep the whole group more self-sufficient, removing reliance on the corrupt State. In this way you'd have to get all your ideas straight. There's nothing like explaining an idea for straightening it out in your own mind.

All that is necessary is to hold on to the 2-Steps as your ultimate goals. But you can implement them bit by bit. Never take on any more than you can chew at any one time. Do not try to run before you can walk. And you must **never let yourself become intimidated** by anyone or anything. If you know your Rights (your heart will tell you what they are), **you must stand your ground**. It does not matter what they say. **They are wrong**. You must always remain reasonably polite, but firm, and be prepared to 'say it like it is'. All that is really important is to understand the techniques of showing them they are wrong. You'll find those methodologies in the *Example Templates*, included in an Appendix. This may be difficult for those with partners who are not fully behind you. In such cases it is probably better not to start what cannot be finished.

Chapter 14: The Principles of the Application of Common Law

It is imperative that you understand them. They are really not hard, because they are based entirely on the Common Sense of peaceful and equitable co-existence.

Under Common Law crimes are, of course, possible. These will have the following components:

1. A description of the Crime, being the act that was criminal (e.g. murder, fraud, etc)

2. A party who was injured - suffered harm, or loss, or was deceived by mischief. This must be a Human Being.

3. Someone who makes this claim. This must be a Human Being. Because only a Human being has a Mind with which to devise a claim. It cannot be 'THE COURT', or 'THE CROWN PROSECUTION SERVICE', etc., because these are not Human Beings, and have no Mind with which to devise the claim.

In summary, therefore, a crime comprises the ACT COMMITTED, the INJURED PARTY, and the CLAIMANT.

In any circumstance, therefore, someone who is being accused of anything at all, can reasonably ask: *"What is the CRIME, who makes the CLAIM, and who is the INJURED PARTY?"*

And these questions will be unanswerable if no Common Law transgression had occurred.

Perhaps it is also essential to point out that a CRIME itself has two components, being the **act** itself, and that the action was **deliberate**. This takes into account genuinely accidental damage, which could not have been reasonably foreseen. In other words, for a crime to be proven, it has to be proved that the transgressor was Guilty of Mind ('mens rea', in Law)

Contracts stem from Common Law. Contracts between two Human Beings. And this is the crux of the 'Freeman business'. And this is why Legalese attempts the subterfuge of defining Partnerships as being equivalent to Human Beings via the Legal Fiction Person construct.

Because, for a Contract to be lawfully-binding (enforceable), it must comprise the four components described in the Chapter on *Promises & Contracts.*

The Principles of the Application of Common Law

The only positive way to avoid entering into a lawfully-binding Contract is to use the Intent component, by stating, up front: "*I do not consent*" (in front of witnesses). Although a better way, which requires no witnesses, is to state it in a letter.

Chapter 15: Fundamental Established Axioms

These are as simplified as I can make them, based on the work of Robert-Arthur: Menard, Mary-Elizabeth: Croft and (to some extent Winston Shrout and Irene-Maus: Gravenhorst). A good 80% of it is their work, tweaked a bit by re-writing, and removing the unnecessary 'God' bits - thereby reducing it to absolute fundamentals.

1) 'Lawful' is what it is all about. 'Lawful' .vs. 'unlawful'. Never get trapped into discussing 'legal'/'illegal'. For example, if you receive back a response, which does not address the substance of your letter, then invariably it will be attempting to inform you of some 'statutory obligation'. Some 'legal obligation' you are assumed to have. (The Respondent will be acting by rote, of course. Because that is the only world inhabited by Organic Robots). You have no statutory or legal obligations, <u>unless you consent</u>. Therefore it is possible to respond along the following lines:

"If your counsel has been advising you on the basis of the fictional world of Legalese and Statutes, then I suggest that you should consider sacking him or her for the perpetration of a fraud. For the simple reason that they are being grossly negligent by ignoring the real world of Common Law, as you will discover quite shortly, should you continue to pursue this matter based in his or her advice.

"I hereby give you Notice that further correspondence in this matter will be charged at £500 per letter from me. If your counsel advises you that I cannot do that, then that would support my contention in the previous paragraph.

"(Ask him if he does it? And ask him what gives him the right to do it. The answer is: Common Law. Then get him or her to re-advise you accordingly. To advise you, for example, that you need to respond in substance, in order to avoid dishonour. And make sure he or she advises you that there is such a thing as a Counterclaim. For harassment. And that I'm not afraid to use it)"

... is the sort of thing. The Solicitor or Lawyer would then respond to the Client: *"Well, I suppose, they may have a point. It might, I suppose, be an idea to humour them? Just in case? I have heard a bit about Common Law, but I'm not terribly au fait with that side of things".*

Send them a copy of this book(?)

2) In order to empower a representative, you must have the power yourself. You cannot give to anyone something you, yourself do not possess. You cannot give them any more than you, yourself, possess. Consequently you can look at anything any representative does, and say:

Fundamental Established Axioms

"I must be entitled to do that myself, without - necessarily - empowering someone else to do it for me".

A good example of this is Peace Officers. If you can empower your representatives (your Government) to create a Peace Force (they would call it a Police Force), then you must have the power to create a Peace Force of your own. After all, where does a People's Government's power come from - if not from the People?

3) In a democracy, 'a majority' does not depend on 'large numbers'. A majority can be as low as **one**. And **that one** must, of itself, (therefore) carry sufficient empowerment to put any motion into practice. (The US Supreme Court has 9 Members. A 5 - 4 majority carries any ruling. That's 'democracy')

4) Consequent to Axiom 3, above, no Government has more power than you do, yourself. **The powers are equal**. The only difference is that your power is Inalienable - it can't be taken away from you - whereas a Government can be replaced by some other set of role players. **Consequently you are 'supreme'**.

5) 'Requesting permission' is the act of a child. 'Licencing' is 'begging for permission' and 'submitting to someone else's will'. Adults do not beg permission for something they are lawfully entitled to do, and prepared to take full responsibility for so doing. Anything for which a licence can be granted must, by definition, be fundamentally lawful (otherwise it would be incapable of being licenced), and there is, therefore, absolutely no need for an adult to 'ask such permission'. The act of 'obtaining a licence' is the act of throwing away a fundamental Right, and substituting a (revocable) privilege instead.

6) 'Registration' of anything transfers superior ownership to the entity accepting the registration. Once an item has been registered, you are no longer the OWNER (even though you will still be paying for the item), but instead you become the KEEPER. This includes cars, houses, children (who become 'wards of the state' by virtue of a birth registration), etc. ('regis ...' = handing ownership to The Crown ... which, by the way, is the British Crown in Temple Bar, and **not** Elizabeth II).

Not convinced? Perhaps you can think of it this way: What is the benefit of registering anything?

Oh! It makes it 'official'! But what, precisely, does that mean? Does registering:

1. Alter the size of anything?

2. Alter the shape of anything?

3. Alter the colour of anything?

4. Alter the value of anything?

No? Well ... what does 'registration' do then? What does 'making it official' do? For you, I mean. For you, the 'registrant'? Not sure? Well, it must do something, because it is - apparently - so important. Surely there is only one possible answer. 'Registering' transfers Ownership. Away from you, and to whoever accepts the registration. What else could it possibly do?

I repeat: *"What else could it possibly do?"* (Please don't say: *"I don't know"*, because you know as much as anyone else).

What are your benefits from having 'registered something'? The only one I can think of is 'freedom from undue & unnecessary harassment'. But that's hardly a benefit, surely? In the case of cars, for example, the 'benefit of registering your car is that you get regular demands for the payment of Road Tax - because you are the Keeper (check your V5, it calls you the Keeper), and no longer the Owner'.

But it is still up to you to pay for everything, including the MOT and all servicing costs. This is a 'benefit'? If this is considered a 'benefit', then it sounds to me like someone is using the wrong dictionary.

What is the benefit of registering a child? So that it can be pumped full of toxic vaccinations while it cannot in any way defend itself? At the time when it must trust you most? (Check the ingredients of vaccines, they will make your hair stand on end. Vaccinations do not work. They are nothing more than toxic).

Registration so your child can be 'treated' by a General Practitioner who is blindly following the rules laid down by the British Medical Association to create nothing more than 'consensus medicine'? Where each one does what all the others do - rightly or wrongly - such that none of them can be picked out and sued for harmful practices? Meanwhile there are Holistic Practitioners who will offer actual cures (without side effects, and as opposed to just 'treatments'). If any of this is news to you, check out the WebSite of the Nurses Movement for Responsibility in Medicine (www.nmrm.org) for more information.

And then, of course, there is the 'benefit' of indoctrination from the age of 5 years. Sorry, I meant 'education'. Not indoctrination? Well, how much of the contents of this book did you learn at school? Did you learn about the Grand Deceptions of Money, Legalese & Religion at school? Or did they just train you to be nothing more than a compliant workhorse, as they did me?

Fundamental Established Axioms

After finishing (let's say) 'schooling', your child will go out to work, trailing his or her National Insurance Number all over the place. This allows your child to be taxed to the hilt. Which is all a complete fraud as the Chapters on Money and Mass Mind Control and Enslavement fully explain.

Registration of cars and children have benefits?

Really?

Registration of your car means the Government owns your car, and you are the Keeper. And you have all the expenses. Registration of your child means the Government owns your child, and you are the Guardian. And you have all the expenses. (But yes, you still get all the love … unless they decide to take your child away from you … which they can, and do, sometimes on the slightest pretext). Registration of your house means the Government owns your house, and you are the Occupier. And you have all the expenses. The Government can take back your house if you don't leave it to a next of kin. The Government doesn't care. It will get it one day. In the meantime you fund all the upkeep.

7) When parts of the Magna Carta were 'transferred' into Statutes what was actually happening was that fundamental Rights were being transferred into **revocable** privileges. Thus they were being watered down. Diffused. Being rendered powerless. However the Magna Carta Statute did not revoke the Magna Carta Peace Treaty, signed by John with the Royal Seal in 1215. A Statute cannot do that. Thus whatever parts were left out of the Magna Carta Statute (notably Article 61, creating the right & duty of Lawful Rebellion), and whatever parts of the Magna Carta Statute have been repealed, the entire original Magna Carta Peace Treaty 1215 stands in perpetuity as an irrevocable foundation of the Common Law.

8) In all cases you are always **being offered a service** - which includes 'benefits' - in the form of privileges. You are always fully entitled to waive such services, and of course you will also be waiving the attendant benefits, as you so choose. Your choice is - ultimately - to either assert your (inalienable) Rights, or accept (revocable) privileges.

9) Law can give rise to a fiction, but a fiction cannot give rise to Law. Consequently a Legal Fiction called THE GOVERNMENT has no power to make Law. It is, in point of fact, **bound by Law** (like everyone else, and including all other Legal Fictions). PARLIAMENT is another Legal Fiction entity. Statutes created by Parliament are not, therefore, the Law. They are 'legislated rules for a Society' and only applicable to the Members of that Society. Join a different Society, and you would be bound by a different set of rules. (If this were not the case it would be

impossible to become, for example, a Freemason and be bound by the rules of Freemasonry). Statutes are nothing more than the Company Policy of THE UNITED KINGDOM CORPORATION, or THE UNITED STATES OF AMERICA CORPORATION, etc. (See 'Society', below)

10) Only a sovereign flesh and blood Human Being, with a living soul, has a Mind. Only something with a Mind is capable of devising a Claim. Legal Fictions are soulless, and do not possess a distinct Mind. They cannot, therefore, in Law, make a Claim.

11) Consequent to the foregoing, and since the Judiciary in a Court de facto derives all its power from colour-of-law/Statutes, then no Court de facto has any power over you as a sovereign Human Being, **in fact** (although, of course, they don't bother to tell you!). A Court de jure is the only kind of court to which you are subject under Common Law, and there are few of those left (unless you insist that the Court operates de jure, by demanding a Trial by Jury. But they will attempt to resist that with every fibre in their 'corporate', soulless, 'bodies'). Courts de jure only tend to exist as the Higher Courts, where (for example) murder trials take place. Nevertheless the Magna Carta gives everyone the Right to Trial By Jury – or: "*... by the law-of-the-Land ...*" which is Common Law, of course.

12) You, and your fellow Countrymen, constitute the entire and total 'wealth' of your country. The resources may be considered as assets, but without you & your fellow Countrymen they are worthless. A field must be ploughed, and seeded, before potatoes will grow. Once grown they must be dug up, bagged, and transported before they can do the worthwhile job of sustaining life. Without the efforts of you, and your Countrymen, **nothing can happen**, and your Country itself is a worthless lump of soil.

13) A Society is, in essence, nothing more than a grouping of like-minded souls, since it is defined as a number of people joined by mutual consent to deliberate, determine and act for a common goal. A Society makes its own rules, and its Members are duty-bound to follow them. Different Societies can exist, having their own unique set of rules. One way of 'choking' the action of a Court de facto is to claim Membership of a Society that only exists in Common Law jurisdiction. The World Freeman Society (Google it) has been set up precisely for this purpose.

14) Contractual Obligation. For any Contract to be lawful it must comprise the following:

A) **Full Disclosure** by both Parties. Neither Party can later claim 'you should have known' if it was not specifically declared at the time of making the Contract.

B) **Equal Considerations** offered by both Parties, this being the subject of the exchange. It must be a sum of money, or an item of value, and must come from a Party's own resources. Both Parties agree that their Consideration is worth (to them) the other Party's Consideration. The Considerations, once agreed, must be fixed – otherwise they cannot remain 'equal'.

C) **Lawful Terms & Conditions** for the Contract, to which both Parties agree. These should rest entirely on Common Law.

D) **Manifestations of Intent** by both Parties, such as 'wet' (handwritten) signatures, or some conduct or performance which shows 'Intent to Contract'.

Even though businesses and officials act as though there is a lawful contract in place, 99 times out of 100 these rules have not been followed. (Maybe it is 999 times out of 1,000 - or even more!). Standing on these four rules, requesting Proofs, is the simplest way of stalemating just about every action that may be taken against you. (See Axiom 16, below)

15. Agreement to Pay. Consequent to Axiom 14, above, all 'payment demands', that could result in court actions against you, can be stopped by 'conditionally agreeing to pay the sum demanded', subject to Proofs that the four rules were followed in the first place. (Make sure you send this letter by registered post, heading it **Notice of Conditional Agreement** and including **'Without Prejudice'** in a suitable place). In almost all cases no Proofs are possible (because the rules were never followed lawfully).

[**Errata, September 7th, Final Edition: 'Without Prejudice'** should nor be used. See Chapter 24]

However, by 'agreeing to pay' you have removed all Controversy. Thus a court action, which is only there to adjudicate on Controversy, cannot take place. If you receive a Summons, you can write back (registered!) with a copy of your Conditional Agreement to Pay, subject to the Proofs being presented. The Court should consider that any further action is 'frivolous', i.e. a complete waste of its time, since there is no Controversy on which it can adjudicate. (The Court may even consider whoever applied to be in contempt). (See Axiom 16, below)

16. *"I feel 'guilty', because I owe the money. I took it and spent it".* ***No, you don't owe a damn thing!*** When taking out the loan, you were 'loaned' back what was yours in the first place. You created the 'money' when you signed the Loan or Credit Application. By doing so, **you gave them** a Negotiable Instrument called 'the money'. They cashed this in(*), and then used that to loan you back your own money. You don't owe a damn thing!

They owe you - an apology at the very least - for applying this confidence trick on you - and for chasing you for something you already gave them!

(* Actually they just could have walked away with your cash. But they didn't, because they are greedy, greedy, greedy, greedy. They knew they could get you to pay everything back, and also to pay them Interest on top of that. **Thus they had already been paid in full once**, when they cashed in on your money, they took a risk by offering it back to you, and reckoned on **being paid twice or even more**, via the Interest. Are you just beginning to feel slightly less sympathetic? If not, I don't know what else to say, except maybe to Google *Money as Debt*, the superb animation by Paul Gringnon, which explains the entire process step by step, and how it all came about, historically).

17. 'Responsibility' .vs. 'Authority'. You can **delegate** Authority, but you can only **share** Responsibility. In other words, if you task (delegate) someone to do something, you still retain the responsibility for getting it done, and for anything that may happen as a result. If, for example, a Police Officer carries out any order, given by a superior, then that officer is personally responsible for what may occur as a result, **and all those up the chain of command are considered accomplices, in Law**.

(That's what the Nuremberg Trials were all about).

Therefore it is important that, if you delegate Authority, you delegate to the right individual or group of individuals. You delegate to an individual who will accomplish the task without come-backs. And who you choose is your choice, and always remains your Responsibility.

18. A Solicitor or Lawyer has his or her **first duty to the Court** & the public, **not to the Client**. In this situation, in Court, they are considered to be an 'adult', and the Client is considered to be 'a ward of the Court'. A ward of the Court is considered to be a 'non-comprehending child'. With good reason, if you think about it. Actually the Client's status is, in essence, that of an 'imbecilic child'. And, furthermore, because the first duty is to the Court, and therefore its jurisdiction, the 'imbecilic child' has immediately tacitly consented to Statute Law jurisdiction in the Legalese world of illusion. (Unless you get this totally straight with the Solicitor or Lawyer at the outset. However you will go a long way before finding a compliant one).

Chapter 16: Signatures

Do not sign anything unless you intend to Contract. This sounds obvious but it is not obvious. Not signing anything includes letters of rebuttal.

The reason is simple. In this day and age counterfeiting your Signature is perfectly possible. And it happens. And has happened.

Obviously the counterfeiting mechanism will not be perfect, but a Human's Signature Mark varies over time.

It is one thing to say, in Court: *"That signature is a forgery"*, but it is another thing to prove it, unless you are prepared to pay the fees of a Handwriting Expert.

It may be that you can show, by means of other correspondence, that you never had any intention to Contract. A Court may, or may not, accept this reasoning. The best thing to do is to not let anyone get a specimen of your Signature.

There are a number of possible tricks. You could get a friend to sign the bottom of a document. This would be a sure way of proving a forgery and consequent perjury.

Another way suggested is to affix a stamp, and sign over the top of it, thereby making it very hard to extract that section of your actual Signature.

Another possibility is to print a complicated graphic as a Signature Box, and make your mark inside it.

Another possibility is to use a Rubber Stamp with some miscellaneous pattern on it.

Finally it is possible to simply not sign it.

Chapter 17: Courts & Proceedings

Before going any further it is necessary to explain the Courts. There are two kinds, known as a 'Court de jure' and a 'Court de facto'. 'De jure' means 'of Justice', thus a Court de jure is a Court of Justice. 'De facto' means 'of fact'. It **is**. It just 'is' (established). But that's it. It is a private concern providing an arbitration service. (Supposedly independent, but with the overall desire - as do all private concerns - to simply make a profit).

A Court of Justice will be operating under Common Law (i.e. will have Common Law jurisdiction). Trials will take place. In front of a Jury, whose verdict is sacrosanct. The Judge is not allowed to sway the verdict of a Jury. If he or she tries, then you would need to intercede. The Jury may return a verdict of: *"Not guilty"* if they consider they would have done the same thing in your shoes at the time, irrespective of what 'the Law' might demand. The Jury would need to be told this by you. These days, it is unlikely that the Judge will explain this to the Jury (it is all part of the Grand Deception, designed to suppress justice in the form of Jury Trials). A Judge will generally explain the law (as he or she sees it!) to the Jury, and not point out that the **true job** of the Jury **is actually to make the Law, in the specific circumstances of the case in hand**. Courts de jure are very rare these days. Only the Highest Courts function 'de jure' and, as I said, they are rarely directed properly.

Generally speaking you will receive Summonses for Courts de facto. You will get very little 'justice' in a Court de facto. Its entire grounding is based on the illusion of money. Hence the possibilities for corruption are in-built and endless. What is a Court de facto? Nothing more than a private Company, publicly trading. You will be able to obtain a Credit Report on it, via Dun & Bradstreet.

Back in the 11th, 12th and 13th centuries these Courts evolved as private businesses, offering the service of supposed-impartial adjudication. For a fee. The idea was to reduce controversies settled at sword-point. It was, however, due to some very strange adjudications (presumably based on backhanders … always the possibility when 'fees' are involved, of course!) that sparked off the ultimate confrontation, in 1215, at Runnymede. There comes a point (does there not?) where 'enough is enough'. I believe we are, yet again, at such a point in the 21st century.

Courts & Proceedings

In a Court de facto there will be three (generally) 'adjudicators' sitting as a 'panel', or 'bench'. They will either call themselves Magistrates or Judges (Judges in the Higher Courts).

A Court de facto does **not** have Common Law jurisdiction. It is only allowed to adjudicate on the basis of Statutes (which are actually Maritime Law). It is, therefore, an Admiralty Court, in fact. In such a Court there will be a Hearing, not a Trial.

If, after having had correspondence with the Organic Robots, they still persist in Court action, you have a number of options. The Court will almost certainly be a Court de facto. You will be able to tell by looking at what you have been accused of breaching. If it is a Speeding or Parking offence, then that will come from a Statute, and not from Common Law.

If you harmed another Human Being, or caused them a loss, or breached the peace, or are accused of defrauding them, then the charge will probably be a Common Law charge, and the best thing you could do would be to fight it normally (plead guilty or not guilty, and place your case in front of a Jury).

Anything else, including when accused of defrauding (say) the State, or any of its Agencies, would be a charge under Statute, and you can fight it by means of the *Example Templates* given in the Appendices. And - where necessary - ultimately claiming Common Law jurisdiction (as explained below).

The steps to take are firstly to rebut the Summons. This is discussed in the Chapter on *Notices, Invitations & Summonses* - the methodology being to initially send your own Notice back to the Court. They are unlikely to respond in substance, which then places the Court themselves in dishonour. And this is something you can point out since, in Law: *"He who dishonours, loses"*.

If it looks like they have ignored your Notice, then you will need to fight.

The next step is then to send the Court copies of all correspondence, pointing out that you have offered Conditional Agreement, and thus you see no Controversy. You also demand that all your correspondence should be placed into the Magistrate's or Judge's evidence, if the Hearing actually goes ahead.

You may get back a reply saying: *"Case withdrawn"*. This will happen only if whoever you are dealing with has a grain of sense, and does not have a brain the size of a pea.

Consequently you will not get that reply if they are all being as stupid as each other. (Organic Robots can be like that, especially in these Common Purpose days).

So it may, ultimately, be necessary to actually attend the Hearing. Primarily to ensure that, if the Hearing goes ahead, and your Common Law claim fails, then your correspondence is read out.

You cannot afford to trust anyone other than yourself.

However, it still may not get to that. If you arrive a half-hour before the time stated, then there will be an Usher or Clerk outside the Court.

Explaining that you are only present in order to make a **Special Appearance**, in order to **establish jurisdiction**, because you will not be crossing the Bar, **into their ship(*)**, and will be: ***"Claiming Common Law jurisdiction*** *and* ***will not be accepting any offers of services, and will be waiving all the benefits"*** is likely to send said person into a tizzy. Especially if you draw attention to the correspondence that you would use as your evidence.

(* It's an Admiralty Court!).

You are likely to be told that all of this: *"Is baseless"*, or: *"Has no legal basis or standing"*. The response is that: *"I absolutely agree that it is legally baseless, however it has ABSOLUTE LAWFUL standing"* and is not, therefore, in any way 'LAWFULLY baseless'. **And that is the important aspect**. **And the only important aspect**.

If told the Magistrates & the Court have 'statutory obligation' of any kind, the response is: *"It may very well be the case that your Company has some statutory obligation as a part of its business practices. However, as a Sovereign Human Being, I am under no obligation whatsoever to accept any services any Company may have on offer, and that includes the Adjudication Service provided by your Company"*.

Obviously: *"What do you mean, we are not a Company!"*, is countered with: *"Oh yes you are. A private Company actively trading. Do you not even know who, or what, you actually work for?"*

You must always remain reasonably polite, but firm, not be intimidated by anyone, or anything, and be prepared to 'say it like it is'. (**You may have to insist**. They. Don't. Like. It. Up 'em!)

The likelihood of this going any further is very small. One likely possibility is that, after consultation with 'a Superior', it has been decided to adjourn the Hearing. (Note: This is before you have stepped into the Courtroom). You could then ask for Travel Expenses, if that's the case.

You are likely to get a letter, within a day or so, saying the case has been withdrawn (they won't tell you why).

If you don't, then you may have to go through the whole rigmarole again, on the Adjournment Date. If the amount on the case is not large, then they have a large incentive to just give up on you, as in: *"What the hell? We can't win every single one! And this one isn't going to be very profitable"*.

Yes, there is a 'wearing down' factor that is on your side.

Finally, however, you may actually end up in Court. In the actual Hearing itself. When you hear your name, you approach the outer reaches of the Court and say: *"I am here making a SPECIAL APPEARANCE in order to ESTABLISH JURISDICTION. I claim my Inalienable Human Right to Common Law jurisdiction, and DO NOT CONSENT TO CONTRACT for any SERVICES you may have on OFFER, and I WAIVE ALL THE BENEFITS"*.

Do not say anything else. If any question is put to you, repeat the exact same mantra.

If you are told that you will be in Contempt of Court if you repeat that mantra once more, then ask: *"Would that be CIVIL CONTEMPT, or CRIMINAL CONTEMPT?"*

Then do not say any more, except to repeat that second mantra if any question is put to you.

If they respond: *"Civil"*, (the most likely) then ask: *"Where is the Contract? I have made no Contract with you. I specifically stated that I refused all your Contractual Offers"*.

They might then change it to: *"Criminal"*, in which case the response is: *"What is the CRIME, who makes the CLAIM, and who is the INJURED PARTY?"*

They might just have a final go: *"The Court (or Crown Prosecution Service, or Ministry of Justice, or whatever) makes the Claim"*, to which the response is: *"You know that only a Human Being can devise a Claim"*.

At this point the Court has completely run out of possibilities, because there is no Injured Party, anyway.

If, on the other hand, the proceedings still continue, make sure your correspondence is read into evidence.

If you eventually lose, then it was a total Kangaroo Court, and they were 'totally out to get you, by hook or by crook'. Whatever you would have done would have had the same result. In this case you would need to appeal via a Judicial Review or present a Case Stated, in order to get the Kangaroo Decision quashed. The very last thing for you to do is to give up. A Higher Court would almost certainly quash it on a technicality.

Freedom Is More Than Just A Seven-Letter Word

A Freedom of Information Request was made to a Magistrates Court in the High Peaks area. The question was posed: *"Are you a Court de jure, or a Court de facto?"* The answer received was: *"We do not understand the question"*.

So, in essence we have the fact that the Courts don't even know what they are, and live in the Legalese world of illusion.

Based on experience, and what has been said above, one possibility might be a conversation with the Clerk or Usher outside the Courtroom (please do not dismiss the likelihood of this, it is more than likely and - anyway - what is there to lose?):

"Excuse me, is this a Court de jure or a Court de facto?"

"I beg your pardon?"

"I asked if this was a Court de jure or a Court de facto?"

"I'm, sorry, I don't know what you mean"

"A Court of Justice, or a Court of Adjudication"

"Well, errr ... I suppose a Court of Justice"

"So will there be a Jury, then?"

"A Jury? No ... there won't be a Jury"

"How can it be a Court of Justice, then?"

"Errr ... well I suppose it must the other kind you mentioned"

"A Court de facto? With Hearings instead of Trials?"

"Oh! Yes ... there will be a Hearing!"

"So it's a Court de facto, then?"

"Yes, that's the case"

"Well why did you tell me it was a Court of Justice, then? Oh, well, never mind, in that case I refuse its offer of the service of arbitration, and I waive all the benefits"

"I beg your pardon?"

"I don't consent to any Arbitration Service. I remain in Common Law jurisdiction. I'm only subject to Courts de jure. Like we all are if we realise it"

"What do you mean ... you are only subject to Courts de jure?"

"What I said. So would you be so kind as to pay my expenses for coming, since I'm here under false pretences, £10 will suffice, and I'll be on my way"

"On your ... what do you mean 'false pretences'?"

"Well, what Common Law have I broken?"

"I don't understand ... I'll have to speak with my Superior ..."

"Yes, that's a good idea. Maybe he knows what kind of a court it is. I have to say that I find it a little alarming that you sit there - doing what you do - and you didn't even know what kind of court it was. I certainly hope your Superior knows ..."

(Comes back)

"We don't need your consent to this Hearing ..."

"I beg your pardon ... did I hear you say you don't need my consent?"

"Yes, we don't need your consent"

"How can that be?"

"Well, I don't really know ... that's what I've been told ..."

"Then please be so kind as to go back to whoever told you that and point out we are all equal under the Law-of-the-Land, and if you don't need my consent, then I don't need you to provide any Arbitration Service"

(Goes away to re-confer ... comes back)

"There seems to be a little problem. Your Hearing has been adjourned for a month"

"Now I beg your pardon!"

"They've adjourned it for a month"

"To give themselves time to turn this into a Court de jure? They can do that in just one month?"

"I don't know about that"

"Well, with all due respect, would you please be so kind as to find out about that? After all, I'm here, the court is here, you are here, your Superior is here, why do we need an adjournment?"

"I'll go and find out"

"Yes, thank you"

(Goes away to re-confer ... yet again ... comes back)

You could very easily be looking at: *"Case withdrawn"*.

There is nothing to stop you having this conversation well before the date of the Hearing. Just go down to the Court and ask the same questions, adjusting what you say accordingly.

Solicitors, Lawyers and Notaries live entirely in the world of illusory Legalese, and almost every sentence they write can, under careful scrutiny, be shown that they are double-thinking, and attempting to compute fiction with fact, totally unsuccessfully. An example I heard of was: *"When you were born your parents gave you a name. They registered your birth, and you are, therefore, Mr. Blah Blah".*

First of all the parents do not register the birth. The Government Agency, known as The Registrar of Birth & Deaths, registers the birth. The parents merely provide the requisite information. The parents merely inform. So strike that one out.

Secondly the Solicitor admits, in the first sentence, that the subject was 'given' a Name, by the parents. That indicates the Flesh & Blood, and the Name, are obviously two totally different things that became attached, following the birth. (There is more about this in the Chapter on *Names*). So here the Solicitor is using Common Sense, without realising it, and desperately trying to draw the fictional conclusion in the second sentence. He is thus completely contradicting himself. Strike two out.

Furthermore, whenever asked to give or confirm your Name and Date of Birth you are expressing hearsay in Court. You only have your parent's and Birth Certificate's word for those two things. You only 'know' these things by hearsay. And hearsay evidence is not allowed in a Court.

So, in essence we have the fact that Judges, Solicitors, Lawyers and Notaries, etc., do not know what they doing, and what they are talking about.

And we have a force of Policymen who do not comprehend the immense difference between Common Law (lawful) and Company Policy (legal).

Is it really any wonder there is so much trouble all round?

Hot off the press, August 2009.

At the time of publication it seems the word has gone round to say there are some people who - when faced with a Court Hearing - claim Common Law jurisdiction, and will not enter the Court proper.

A number of incidents have given rise to this assumption. For example, Defendants who remain in the Public Gallery, saying: *"I am here to make a Special Appearance, in order to establish jurisdiction. I claim Common Law jurisdiction and do not accept your offers of adjudication services. And I waive all the benefits"* ... are told: *"You must come forward, and stand here, and identify yourself correctly".*

Why would this be? Why does one need to stand in a 'designated place' and 'identify themselves correctly'?

The answers are, of course, that the 'designated place' is on board their 'ship'. And 'correct identification' means 'accepting responsibility as the

Legal Fiction Person, by virtue of admitting to the Legal Fiction Name on their paperwork'.

It can't really mean anything else.

If one chooses not to obey these instructions, it appears that the Courts have been instructed to proceed anyway, in absentia of the Legal Fiction Person being present. After a short retirement (usually) the Magistrates and the Clerk return and say: *"Liable person not present"*.

This is really good, isn't it? So much for 'justice', then! Before the Hearing starts, the 'person' is already condemned as 'liable'!

However this is a bit of a double-whammy - back on the Clerk of the Court. Because, if one is sitting in the Public Gallery, then one is certainly 'present in the room'. Not present on the 'ship', of course, but present in the room to hear what has been said.

Consequently it would be possible to respond: *"In that case, since I'm present to hear it, you have declared that I, the Human Being, am not liable - any more than any of you are liable. Thus, if anything untoward should happen to me, for example any Common Law trespass upon me, or my property, I can hold you all personally responsible, can't I? You can sit in your fictional ship, but I can hear you. The truth is that no liable person will board your fictional ship, and will not accept your fictional adjudication. Which is precisely what I have already said by claiming Common Law jurisdiction. You have no jurisdiction over me as a Human Being, and you might as well admit it"*.

At the time of writing, we await their response to that. To date no-one, who has been placed in that position, has responded in that manner. This is due, in total, to them not thinking about it on the spur of the moment.

However, it is nothing more than Common Sense.

After all, they are up against a serious problem, which is that it is impossible to adjudicate between Fictions (Persons/Corporations) and Reality (Humans). It is only possible to adjudicate between Fictions OR between Humans. (Of course, in the former case, the adjudication is: *"Is this fiction more fictional than that fiction?"*).

One reaction we have seen is to 'call the police'. The rebuttal to this is: *'If you need to involve the police, then you've lost the argument, haven't you? You are, in effect, saying that 'might is right'. Is that not so? What other reason could you possibly have? I'm not causing any violence nor breaching any peace. The fact is you are simply reaching for 'muscle', when the honest thing would be to admit that you've lost the argument. You are acting thoroughly dishonourably and disreputably, and that is demonstrated by your own actions"*.

Hot off the press, September 2009.

While, on the one hand, the content of this book is true, the 'powers that be' do not give up without a fight. In the front line are the Organic Robots who simply 'operate by the book'. So here are some examples of how to stop Kangaroo Courts.

Letters written to Organic Robots, based on the Templates included in the Appendix, are 'outside the realm of their Operation Manuals'. Therefore they simply do not know what to do with your letters. So they ignore them. In fact you'll discover, as you try Lawful Rebellion, you will either be ignored, or responded to by repetition of your so-called 'Statutory obligations'.

The point is here that by operating on the Freeman Principles, as described in this book, you will have built up all the evidence you actually need … IN LAW.

The trouble is that, when (eventually) 'invited to their place of business in order to be made the offer of their adjudication services' (i.e. Summonsed), you will be railroaded into submission - if you do not know how to guard against this happening.

Most Summonses will be to Hearings (Note: Not Trials) that will take place in a Magistrate's Court. The Magistrates are not trained in either 'legal' or 'lawful'. The Clerk of the Court will have extensive 'LEGAL training', and is often referred to as "The Magistrate's Legal Advisor". However he or she will most probably have long forgotten any 'LAWFUL training' (if s/he ever had any) - in the desperate struggle to 'slap down as many miscreants as possible' via the Conveyor Belt of the Magistrates Court. So it would be possible to ask: *"Yes, I can see you have a Legal Advisor, but who is your LAWFUL Advisor?"*

A real example is that, of 178 Summonses issued for one day, only 3 people turned up for their Hearing. And this is what 'they' expect. And 'they' expect to deal with the 175 (who were hoping that it would 'all go away if they didn't turn up') by simply rubber-stamping the claims made by the Plaintiffs (e.g. the Council, for Council Tax).

(There is an argument that, if the mechanisms were fair and above board, and everyone knew their Rights, then more Defendants would turn up to challenge the claims made against them. This is one of the reasons why 'they' cannot afford for you to know your Rights. Because you would destroy the Conveyor Belt).

So, what can you do to break the Conveyor Belt? Well, the answer to that is to know how it operates, and to throw spanners into the works, and uncover sufficient grounds for an Appeal. There will be plenty of material to choose from because, fundamentally, the Conveyor Belt only works by cutting corners. So don't allow these corners to be cut, and/or note whenever they are.

Here are some (real, I assure you) examples (as witnessed by me, personally):

1. They will insist that you 'identify yourself correctly'. This will take the form of you accepting your Legal Fiction Name, Date of Birth, and your Address.

   Even though you may state that you are: *"XXX: of the YYY family, as commonly called"*, they will normally insist that they will refer to you by your Legal Fiction Name. They will claim this is a 'courtesy' but, of course, it immediately places you under their jurisdiction if not constantly challenged. The way around this is to ask: *"How would you wish to be addressed?"* They will say: *"You call me 'Your Worship'"*. So you can say: *"If that is your wish, then I will address you as 'Your Worship', as a common courtesy to you. Now, I expect you to reciprocate by addressing me the way I wish, which is by calling me XXX ... and not 'Mr. YYY' ... since I have already told you I consider the latter to be discourteous"*.

   Oh boy ... are they in trouble now ... because you have brought them back to the bedrock of Common Law - addressing you as a Human Being! And, not only that, with all this argy-bargy going on, they could easily forget to insist on confirmation of your Date of Birth and Address!

   When asked for your Date of Birth, you can say: *"Is hearsay allowed then?"* They will say: *"No"*. You can then say: *"I am only aware of my Date of Birth because I was told by my parents, so consequently the answer to that question is hearsay from me. You would need to ask my parents, specifically my mother, to confirm my Date of Birth"*.

   They will be spitting blood.

   But note ... they will still continue. However you now have grounds for an Appeal, because they continued without properly identifying who they were proceeding against.

2. Another major stumbling block, for them, is to insist that you take an Oath. This is generally a waste of time because they won't let you say very much. HOWEVER THAT'S THE WHOLE POINT IN YOUR FAVOUR!

   They will be very careful to choose your Oath in accordance with your 'religion'. (One thing to try ... which has not been tried ... is to say: *"My religion is very personal to me, and it is my business, not yours"*. This would tend to give them a problem).

However, the 'biggie' is that - whatever Oath you take … you will need to swear to: *"… tell the truth, the WHOLE truth … etc"*.

You can argue: *"I cannot swear to tell the WHOLE truth, because I do not know everything there is to know. There is a Bible over there. If I knew the WHOLE truth my name would be in it"*. (This has been done. It confuses!)

They will overcome this by agreeing that 'the WHOLE' truth is only that which concerns the matter at hand. However this kind of filibustering makes them annoyed, and therefore they make mistakes.

And, anyway, they will stop you from saying very much because - as soon as you open your mouth to defend yourself - they cannot let that happen! The objective is to 'process you via the Conveyor Belt' … not to let you defend yourself.

So you need to point this out, either in the Court, or via an Appeal (if they still take no notice): *"You have insisted that I swear an Oath to tell the truth, and then you stop me, running rough-shod over me, when ever I try to do that in order to provide my defence. Not allowing me the FULL opportunity to defend myself, as I see fit, is grounds for an Appeal - irrespective of any decision you may come to"*.

3. They may refuse to let you ask questions (cross-examine) the claims made against you. I have seen this happen. Uh-uh! Grounds for Appeal! It is your Right, in Law, to cross-examine all claims made against you.

All in all you will certainly end up with grounds for an Appeal - on the basis that you were not allowed the chance to defend yourself. (It was called a Hearing, but no-one was 'listening'!) An Appeal costs £75 in the UK, and is a pretty simple form to fill in.

It is, however, quite essential that your Appeal is supported by as many Witness Statements as possible. Have a couple of friends, taking notes, in the Public Gallery.

An Appeal can get the judgment set aside, and the case thrown back to the Magistrates Court. But the second time they'll think twice about ignoring you.

Chapter 18: Liability & The Ultimate Sanctions

The vast majority of 'offences' (they are not actually 'offences', but 'Statute violations', of course) involve 'money'. Specifically: *"The non-payment of it"*.

The Chapter on *Money* explains how it ***does not*** exist in reality, and is nothing more than a Belief System. For this reason the most that can ever be extracted from you is 'belief in something you value', in other words your Credit Rating, or your Liberty.

While the Monetary System is king, a Credit Rating can be assumed to have value. However, I have to say that, in my own case, I paid off my Credit Card in the early 1980s (ACCESS Card, if you can remember them), and cut it up. I did this because I realised I was on a hiding to nothing.

And I've never used a Credit Card since (even though I've been constantly bombarded with junk mail offering them to me).

But that's me. However, it does explain why I, personally, have no idea what my Credit Rating is, and I really don't care. It's not something I consider to have any value. If I want something, I wait until I can afford it, and buy it. It is as simple as that.

But that did not stop the Inland Revenue from placing me in (what they called) 'Notional Debt', and proceeding against me into bankruptcy (because I did not consider I owed them anything). And it did not stop the Margaret Thatcher Government from proceeding against me, and placing me in prison for refusing to pay her Poll Tax.

So I write all this on the basis of two personal experiences. Firstly, being made bankrupt and losing any Credit Rating I had. And secondly, spending time in prison and losing my Liberty for a while.

And, having actually experienced all that, I firmly believe NONE of it would have happened if I had known then, what I know now: The Freeman Principles. I am **absolutely positive** I could have stopped both actions against me, dead in their tracks. I know what was said at the time, because I was there. And I now know what I could have said, but didn't - entirely due to lack of knowledge.

Even without this knowledge I did – in point of fact – have two 'successes'. Guided purely by Common Sense I fought both by simply not co-operating. The result was that the Local Council never bothered me again (because, I presume, they had come to realise it wasn't worth the effort … after all I did tell them that on a number of occasions), and the Inland Revenue never bothered me again, for (I assume) the same, or similar, reason. Which proves, to me at least, that when they operate by rote they may win the battle, but they don't win the war.

However, any procedure against you is always in two stages:

1. To establish Liability, and make a corresponding Court Order against you for the amount demanded;

2. Failure to pay the amount demanded, within the stated timescale, invokes a new Summons to demand that you be placed into bankruptcy, or into prison. Which of these demands is made, depends on the circumstances (the Statutes).

In the case of Council Tax, for example, they will demand a prison sentence for non-payment. The sanction being to take away your Liberty. This is because it would be pointless making you bankrupt ... because they would have no means of making any further demands on you until the bankruptcy expires. (And we can't have that, can we!). Until this **subsequent** Hearing has taken place **no prison sentence has been passed on you**, and so there is no way you could actually be carted off to prison. There has to be a sentence passed before they can do that.

In this case, which is a Civil Offence, you can extricate yourself from the whole situation at any time by paying up. Even if you get as far as prison. They will take the length of the sentence, and divide it into the amount, and come up with 'an amount per day incarcerated'. As each incarcerated day passes, that amount is written off. The remainder will always buy you out. On the last day of your sentence it has all been written off, and you are free once more. (There is no parole for a Civil Offence).

In the case of failure to pay, for example, Income Tax, the likelihood is that they would go for bankruptcy. The idea being that they can take your house, to pay off their 'Notional Debt' ('notional', because 'money' is an illusion). They would tend not to worry about the fact that they could not grab anything from you for a while (i.e. until the bankruptcy has been discharged), on the basis of creaming as much as possible this one-time.

'Long-sightedness' is not one of their stronger points. (Otherwise they wouldn't be doing their job in the first place!). If you co-operate with the Official Deceiver (Receiver), then a bankruptcy is auto-discharged after 3 years. (But they won't bother to tell you, quite probably). (It may even be 2 years by now).

Liability & The Ultimate Sanctions

However, the overall point here is the Second Phase. Either the Incarceration Petition or the Bankruptcy Petition. Nothing can happen to you until this Second Phase has been successfully accomplished by whomsoever is making the demand.

All too often people do not realise what is actually going on, and what is happening, and that there are these two, distinct, phases. And that both can be challenged by Common Law jurisdiction. If the Liability Petition is dismissed because the Court is 'de facto', and does not have Common law jurisdiction, then the Ultimate Sanction Phase **cannot occur**.

Chapter 19: The Law-of-Waters

In the Chapter on *Common Law* it was explained that Common Law is the Law-of-the-Land. It is the **only** Law-of-the-Land. And the only Law that needs to be obeyed on dry land. It fully defines peaceful co-existence within its principles. Nothing can go wrong where everyone adheres to the Law-of-the-Land.

Nothing else is necessary. Adherence to Common Law gives everyone total freedom, provided they remain honourable, and is capable of coming down like a ton of bricks on anyone who deviates from honourable, peaceful, co-existence.

So, what the hell has Parliament been doing, then? Since it was all sorted out in the 11th, 12th and 13th centuries?

What a bloody good question!

The answer is that, driven by the Banksters, it has been very slowly, and in the most subtle manner, ingraining the Grand Deceptions. It has been doing this by fully-utilising the gullible nature of Mankind in general.

It could be argued that while the Law-of-the-Land sorts out what happens on dry land, but what happens on water? Don't we need a Law-of-Waters, to take account of the high seas?

Common Sense should tell anyone that the answer is possibly: *"No"*. That the Common Law still works perfectly well on the high seas, because it fundamentally addresses the Human Condition (honour, dishonour, etc) and Humans on the high seas should still remain honourable.

One the other hand there are such things a Pirates, and Salvage, and also different Cultures, and so on. And you can't reasonably expect Pirates to be honourable, and you can't expect to impose your own Law-of-the-Land on to some other culture's Law-of-their-Land. There will be remarkable similarities, but there may be Religious differences (which they have to contend with, poor souls, and you do not).

So it is reasonable to assume that a Law-of-Waters - which needs to be fully International, contending with the aspirations of all different Cultures - is something that needs to be created and mutually agreed.

Sure, that's all very fine & dandy. It's fine to create some Law applicable on waters ... but to impose that same Law on dry land? Oh, come on! No-one would fall for that one, would they?

The Law-of-Waters

Errr ... well ... yes, by subterfuge everyone fell for that one, and can be most vociferous in supporting the irrationality! Try explaining to a Policeman that he or she swore, on Oath, to uphold the Law-of-the-Land. And, by bleating on about Statutes, he or she is imposing the Law-of-Waters on dry land. The fact that the Police have a duty to understand this, and are grossly negligent if they do not - actually committing serious crimes if they do not - is something that passes completely under their radar.

However before you, the Reader, get the impression that I have an axe to grind with regard to Policemen, it might be an idea to correct that assumption.

When in the course of their duties, they uphold the Law-of-the-Land, in accordance with their Oath of Service, they are acting as Peace Officers. In that role I have as much admiration and respect for them as anyone else. Someone needs to do that job. Someone, some group, some force, needs to impose the Principles of Common Law on those who choose to act outside its boundaries. This is for my protection, as well as everyone else.

It is only when they exceed their jurisdiction, and the authority vested in them via their Oath of Service, that I (and most, by Common Sense, I think) have a problem with the way they act. Just the mere act of stopping and questioning someone, without lawful excuse, is vastly exceeding their Common Law jurisdiction, and that is without considering their involvement in traffic (for example).

On the other hand they do things that I would not wish to do. Picking up torn limbs resulting from road traffic accidents, for example. I salute them, and all the Emergency Services, in that respect.

Acting as Peace Officers is what they are paid to do. I have no problem with that, and welcome it. Acting as Company Policy Enforcement Officers (Policymen), enforcing the Law-of-Waters on dry land, and not realising it, and making absolutely no attempt to realise it, is where they have no authority, no jurisdiction, and are behaving in a grossly negligent manner.

That's where the problem arises for me. And furthermore I suggest that, deep down within their Common Sense, most people feel the same, without actually being able to put their finger on it. So now you know.

When acting as Policymen, they are enforcing the Company Rules of a Company you did not even realise you were working for. No wonder you were confused!

Common Law provides the uninhibited Right to Travel. Actually across National Boundaries **without the need for any kind of Passport**, as it happens.

Common Law says the following are crimes: Injuring someone, or causing them loss.

If you are travelling at 90 mph on a Motorway, and you get from A to B, what injury have you caused? What loss have you caused? What crime have you committed? Answer: None.

Ah! Ah! Ah! The Policymen will say: *"But you could have hurt someone! So there! Can't have you possibly hurting someone! Need to book you. Just doing our job!"*

Firstly if you pick up a knife, to cut a sandwich, you could easily hurt someone, if you dropped it. You could hurt yourself, or someone standing near you. Has no-one ever accidentally dropped something? No? Never happened?

For crying out loud! Give over! The **potential** for harm is ever present. 24/7! **The potential**. But, because most of us actually know what we are doing, the potential doesn't normally turn into a reality.

If the potential ever turns into reality, then we have, indeed, committed a crime and the Law should, indeed, be brought to bear on us. That's precisely what the Law-of-the-Land is for! To rein in those who cause harm or loss to others, due to irresponsibility.

But going from A to B at 90 mph is not irresponsible. If it is, then going from A to B at 70 mph is almost as irresponsible. What's the difference? 20 bloody mph! Duh!

Most people understand this by Common Sense. That's why you can be doing 70 mph on a UK Motorway, and cars whizz by you. No-one is particularly concerned. I'm certainly not. People are just relying totally on their own Common Sense, and basically saying: *"Sod the stupidity of Statutes"*.

It's a form of 'voting with your feet'. **You always have that vote**.

(If this doesn't tell the UK Parliament, and its jobsworth Policymen, 'something', I'm not sure what ever will. Actually I think it does. None of the cameras seem to work, and on a 4-hour journey recently, I did not see one Policyman).

Statutes are the Company Policy of THE UNITED KINGDOM CORPORATION. They are the Law-of-Waters being applied on dry land. That's OK if you consent. But not, if you don't! Various other names are the same thing: Law Merchant, Commerce Law, Equity Law,

The Law-of-Waters

Fleet Law, Maritime Law … you-name-it Law … just various speciality flavours of the Law-of-Waters.

In point of fact there are only two jurisdictions: Common Law and the Uniform Commercial Code. And they co-exist side-by-side. The Uniform Commercial Code applies worldwide, and determines what happens when transactions in Sales of Goods (or a Sales of the Leases of Goods) takes place. That's it. **'Goods' must be movable**.

Consequently Real Estate transactions (they are not 'goods', because they are not movable), and **all Services** fall under Common Law, the Law-of-the-Land. Therefore the Service provided by the Courts and the Police should be one of Peace Keeping under Common Law principles, and nothing more.

It's pretty easy to see why this should come about. The Law-of-Waters, as a Uniform Commercial Code (worldwide) provides Trading Standards for Goods moved between Nations … over intervening seaways. But how on earth could Uniform Commercial Standards be applied to Services, taking place on dry lands, but split across a seaway? How can diners be located in England, while the waiters (providing the Service) be located in, say, France? The only thing applicable to the manner in which those Services are provided, is the Law-of-the-Land (the customs & traditions) within which the restaurant, the diners, the kitchen staff and the waiters are all located.

Returning to water's connotations for a moment, in anticipation of our acquiescence to be duped, and to remain duped, by the application of the Law-of-Waters on dry land, many words in common usage have been adopted. All have associations with water.

Banks = the two sides of a river, which contain the flow of water, the current. Which lends itself to the word 'currency' to determine the flow of 'money'.

The idea that, when your mother's waters broke, you came down the Birth Canal, and can therefore be considered to be a small 'ship'. Because of this you were given a Berth Certificate (although, to hide this, they write it 'Birth', but the pronunciation is exactly the same), because you can be considered to be a small ship 'at berth'. A 'berth' being the place where a ship is moored.

If you are called into a Court, you will be expected to stand in the Dock. A Dock is also another name for where a ship is moored. The basic idea is that, if a ship is impounded (in a Dock), then the Owner will appear to sort the situation out. This is synonymous with you, as a Human Being, being the Owner of your Legal Fiction 'ship'. And when you 'appear to sort the situation out' they can have your body, and do what they like with it. For example, cuff you and send you to prison, should they decide there is a necessity to do that.

More 'water' association comes from the 'ship-associated' words in our language: Citizenship, Relationship, Courtship, Ladyship, Lordship, Worship (Warship? Whoreship? Actually from Worthship ... but at all seems to amount to the same thing, from what I have seen), Ownership, etc.

There are just far too many co-incidences for these water-associations to be accidental, or random in any way. Indeed, even giving people the pseudo-title 'Officer', is indicative of a ship's personnel.

And that's the way it is.

Chapter 20: Names

"S*ticks and stones may break my bones, but names will never hurt me*". So they say. ***If only that were true*** and, by the time you have read this Chapter, you will understand why I say that.

For the simple reason **you are not your Name**. Your Name was 'given' to you ... usually by your parents. But, if you think hard about it, what - precisely - is a Name?

It is a word. Or, more specifically, a group of words. It consists of the word you were 'given' by your parents (they may have 'given' you more than one), and the name of a family into which you were born i.e. your Family Name.

These are nothing more than **words**. They can be written on paper, and can be sounded by someone speaking. If you hear your name spoken, or you see it written, you **assume** you must respond to it. You assume You, Your Human Self, Your Flesh & Blood, Your Sovereign Soul ... must respond to it. **This is a mega-deception**.

Do you not see an enormous difference between Your Human Self, Your Flesh & Blood, Your Sovereign Soul ... and some marks made on a piece of paper? Or sound pressure waves in the air?

No? Well, let's have another go then. Have you ever heard of a Deed Poll? I would guess you probably have. What does it do? It allows you to **change** your Name. To any collections of words you choose. You are saying: *"My Human Self, My Flesh & Blood, My Sovereign Living Soul, will henceforth only respond to this new collection of words, whether written or spoken"*.

That's what a Deed Poll does. And this could only happen if it were possible to DETACH one set of words to respond to (your original Name), and to ATTACH an alternative set of words to which you henceforth respond (your newly-chosen Name).

'Names' are attached! They are attached to flesh and blood, purely for convenience.

Imagine a family with three children. The parents decided not to bother to name them. So, when one child is naughty, the parent shouts: *"Stop doing that!"* All three would turn to look, to see which child the parent was looking at. He or she would then have to say: *"Do you mean me?"*

I think you will find that, a long, long, time ago (in a far-off galaxy?) it was decided that - for convenience - fleshes and bloods should be told

"Listen: Whenever I, or anyone else, says this word, I mean you. OK?" And the child would - eventually - comprehend. Of course, it isn't done like that in practice. It's done the same way we do with domestic pets. Repetition. So they get used to the sound. But the practical convenience, behind the process, is exactly the same.

Why is this so important? Well, simply because your Government thinks your Name is the same as You. (Well, it probably doesn't really, but it always acts as though it does, so you never figure out the difference. And it certainly doesn't inform you of the difference. Did they tell you this at school?).

Every letter you receive is addressed to YOUR NAME. Get it? Addressed to your Name. Not to Your Human Self. Because Human Selves are born 'nameless'. We are not born with a Name tattooed on our foreheads, are we?

This is why your name is actually a Legal Fiction Name. If anyone writes to you, or calls you, using that Name, then you are perfectly entitled to ignore it, or respond: *"'Scuse me, are you talking to me? If you are, then I'm commonly called dah-de-dah".* In my case it's: *"'Scuse me, are you talking to me? If you are, then I'm commonly called Veronica".* And when they continue: *"Yes, Ms. Chapman, I ...",* I interrupt by saying: *"I just told you I'm commonly called Veronica. 'Ms. Chapman' is a Legal Fiction. I am Human and real. I am not fictional, legal or otherwise, as you must surely be able to see?"*

Within their jurisdiction, they can only address your Legal Fiction Name. So. They. Do. Not. Like. It. Up 'em!

Maybe you 'get it' now?

What's in a Name? Everything, baby! EVERYTHING!

Forced to carry an ID Card, You & Your Name are being glued together. Forced to have a microchip implanted, You and Your Name are one and the same thing.

And there is something else of considerable importance. If, in a Court, you are asked to confirm your Name (and Date of Birth), **you cannot**.

You cannot for the simple reason that any knowledge you have is **hearsay**. You would be confirming only what your parents told you. They could have lied about these things, for all you know. Sure, they probably didn't, but how do you know? Sure, you were around at the time ... but not in the position of understanding what was going on! Hearsay is not allowed in a Court, and you can remind them (politely!), explaining that the best you could do would be to repeat, as hearsay, what your parents told you.

Chapter 21: Orders

If you go into a shop that sells curtains, and place an order for some curtains, do you expect to pay? The answer is: *"Yes"*. If you place an order with a Mail Order firm, do you expect to pay commensurate with receiving the goods? The answer is: "*Yes*".

An Order is chargeable! The amount to charge is dependent on the one who carries out the order. The Mail Order firm, and the shop, set their rates. You decide whether or not you are prepared to pay that amount before you place any order.

If someone gives you an order (e.g. a PCSO, Policyman, or a Magistrate), you can say: "*Is that an order?*". If the answer is: *"No"*, then you can say: *"In that case I respectfully decline to provide that service"*.

If the answer is: "*Yes*", you can say: "*In that case, since an order is chargeable, I will charge you £50,000 for carrying it out. Are you prepared to pay?*"

I leave you, dear Reader, to guess what the answer will be. If they are silly enough to agree, in front of witnesses, then you have a Lawful Contract with them (a Lien). So, it is possible to remind them: "*Based on the fact that you are agreeing to a lawfully enforceable Contract, would you like the chance to re-consider?*"

(I think you'll find they generally tend to re-consider).

Chapter 22: Laws, Regulations, Guidelines & Sovereignty

I'm the Legal Fiction, baby ... now here's the twist ... I ... don't ... exist! (with apologies to the Bonzo Dogs, featuring the late Viv Stanshall). Before going anywhere in this morass, we need a few basics.

There are two fundamental kinds of 'Law': Natural and Man-made. Let's characterise them. I think you might agree there are three main characteristics in each case.

Natural Laws or the Laws of Nature, Science, etc.

1) Mankind does not make them. Mankind observes them & their effects, then enumerates and evaluates them; in most cases being able to devise mathematical formulae to express them, utilise them and inter-utilise i.e. apply them. Examples: The Law of Gravity (Newton's Laws), Boyle's Law, Maxwell's Laws, Charles' Law, Ohm's Law, etc.

2) They apply universally and unilaterally without fear or favour.

3) There is no penalty for breaking them because they cannot be broken.

Man-made Laws, Acts, Statutes, etc.

1) Mankind does make them. Mankind changes them in accordance with its own desires, wishes, needs, etc. Mankind can wipe them away (repeal them) at the stroke of a pen.

2) They are applied by Courts of Law. They are not applied equally because they always depend on 'judgment'. It is often said: *"There is one law for the rich and one law for the poor"*.

3) There is always a penalty for breaking them because they can be broken if one is prepared to accept the consequences.

Stated that way I submit it is possible to see that the two kinds are **exact opposites**. Each characteristic is the **exact inverse** of the other.

And yet we use the same word – 'Law' – to describe them both!

So what happens? The latter become psychologically imbued with the characteristics of the former!

So: *"I've got to pay it ... because it's the Law"* takes on the same characteristics as: *"If I jump off this cliff I will fall downwards"*.

Actually, in summary, the most important difference between the two is a simple word: 'consent'.

If you jump off the cliff you will fall downwards. The falling does not require your consent. It will happen. Your consent is whether or not you actually jump – or whether or not you are standing on the edge of the cliff at all.

In the second case (*"I've got to pay …"*) your consent is very much required. You have to consent to reach for your chequebook and fill in a cheque – and post it, etc.

However, the essential point being made here is that even if you do not consent to write that cheque, your consent is still needed in all stages of: *"What may happen if the bill is not paid"*.

Your 'consent' is built-in as an essential to the system of Man-made Laws, Statues, etc. Your consent is irrelevant to the Laws of Nature.

The Law of Gravity is set in tablets of stone, and operates whether someone has written it down or not. You will have been led to believe, throughout your entire life, that Statutes are equally set in tablets of stone. They are **not**. They are nothing more than Company Policy written down using ink on paper.

The trick, the Grand Deception, is to create the Legal Fiction Person for you, and to address everything 'statutory or officious' to that fiction, using a Legal Fiction Name … which is sufficiently similar to what you would naturally respond (i.e. to *"What you are commonly called"*). Thereafter you have become tricked into accepting a role in this: *"All the world's a stage, and we are just players of bit parts"*.

To do this they get you to pretend to be what you are not. But they call this 'thing' something you will naturally assume that you are. And they know that you will naturally make this assumption. And they utterly rely on it. Only a system that is utterly evil and thoroughly corrupt - without any possibility of redemption - could have dreamed up this dooley, which is fully described in the Chapters devoted to *Legalese* and to the *Legal Fiction Person.*

From the point of view of you, yourself, the Human Being with the living soul, Man-made Laws or Statutes can be treated as guidance and nothing more. They are not Laws. They are Regulations. As far as you are concerned they can be considered to be Guidelines … but that's only if you choose to consider them that way. It is perfectly possible to reject any or all of them, as not having your consent.

And this leads to the idea of 'sovereignty'.

Freedom Is More Than Just A Seven-Letter Word

We often hear that: *"All are created equal"* – and, of course, we are. Every baby arrives (basically) the same way, and has the exact same needs. It doesn't matter whether you are born in the Queen's Hospital or in a Traveller's Van.

But, what does: *"All are created equal"* translate to? In practice? How can everyone be created equal?

The only way is by some standardised mechanism. This is usually stated as: *"In the image of the Creator"*, which implies that each created individual is a clone from the same model. Even if you don't believe in a Creator (as I don't – I believe in a Universal Life Force, Universal Consciousness – you can call it God if you like), it still amounts to the same thing – just using different rhetoric.

Of course: *"All are created equal"*, thus no-one should be treated differently from anyone else.

But I am not you, and you are not me. (That's arguable, actually, if we are all derived from One Consciousness)

So that's a big difference. But there is a big similarity: We are individually responsible for our individual actions. And that's one of the basic tenets of life.

And the only way that I can be responsible for my own actions, and – at the same time – you be responsible for your own actions is if we are both **sovereign individuals**, and equal in all cases (*"In the same image"*).

I'm sorry if I lost you. Think of it this way. You say your Country is 'sovereign'. What does that mean? It means it is equal to all other countries. It means it has the right to govern itself, without external interference. Your country considers itself to be equal to all other countries.

The same applies to you. Why not? A 'country' is only a collection of individuals who, together, make up the population.

You must be as sovereign as your Country. And so must everyone else in your Country. Otherwise how can your Country be sovereign? Where does your Country's sovereignty come from, then?

FACT: You are a sovereign Human Being by birth, because **your spirit is sovereign**. You are responsible for your own actions – certainly after the 'age of majority'.

You have two choices: You can take your sovereignty, and wield it. Or you can, by consent, give it away. So now we are back to 'consent'. And we are also back to 'person' because – by consenting to wear the Legal

Laws, Regulations, Guidelines & Sovereignty

Fiction Person overcoat, you tacitly accept the jurisdiction of any Statute Law/Regulation/Guideline you may be accused of violating.

Chapter 23: The Hive Mind

We must get out of the habit of falling into the 'Hive Mind Trap' constantly and consistently. Almost, it seems, with every breath we take. Perhaps one of the best ways of expressing the Hive Mind is by example. When asked: *"Why do you do that?"*, a Hived Mind response is: *"It's what we do now. That's the way we do it"*. End of story. End of conversation. End of discussion. End of argument.

No ... it's not the end of the discussion! Nothing like! The original question is not answered by that response. However, it is generally the only answer you'll get from some Organic Robot who has a Hive Mind.

In other words that's a Hive Mind answer.

But there are also Hive Mind questions. For example: *"How do we do this officially?"*, is that kind of question. The question should have been: ***"What's the best way to do this honourably?"***

I mean, what has 'officially' got to do with anything?

The Hive Mind is ingrained into our psyche due to the indoctrination we suffer during childhood. It comes from our parents and schooling. It comes from these sources because they were similarly indoctrinated - as opposed to being properly educated - during their own childhoods.

"What would the neighbours think?" was a perennial favourite of my own mother. I used to tell her: *"I don't give a shit what they think. That's their problem, not mine"*.

(I can only presume I was born a rebel).

I hated school ... due to its Hive Mind attitude. Although I couldn't put my finger on it at the time. I just knew it was all wrong 'somehow'.

A Builder can make a house. A house cannot make a Builder. The Builder is 'above' the house.

A Human Being can make a Law. The Law cannot make a Human Being. The Human Being is 'above' the Law. It has to be that way. And the Law has already been made. Centuries ago. Although there were attempts beforehand, a major boost, to codify it properly, occurred in 1215.

When we are in Hive Mind mode we are not 'above' anything. Our mentality is 'below' the situation. We are looking upwards, and wondering: *"How to do this officially?"* We are looking for 'guidance from above'.

The Hive Mind

The correct attitude is to use our Common Sense, and to take an honourable course of action. Then our mentality is right where is should be: **Above** the situation at hand.

I'm often told that many people want 'to be led'. This argument can - to some extent - be countered by wondering whether or not their childhood indoctrination has left them in that state? And whether or not, if they had been educated instead of indoctrinated during that period of their lives, perhaps they would not want to let the Government (and it propaganda arm, called 'The Media') do all their thinking for them?

But I'm obviously out on a limb with that answer. Simply because I'm unable to prove it, of course. My Common Sense tells me … but that's all.

But my Common Sense also tells me that - even if the vast majority would not want to be led by the nose had they been properly educated - then there is still the possibility that some would want it that way.

OK. Fine. Let them be sheep, and led by the nose - by some nannying Big Brother-style Government.

But don't include me in that, sunshine! Because I don't accept being treated as a 'lowest common denominator'. And, I believe, there are millions of us who object to being treated like that.

And we have a voice.

And that's what this book is all about.

Chapter 24: Without Prejudice

You will find that letters considered to be 'of importance' may include the words: *"Without Prejudice"* somewhere prominent, either at the top or the bottom. And you can use this yourself on correspondence you create.

What, actually, does this mean?

Well, it doesn't mean that whoever writes it is 'not prejudiced against the addressee'. And it is important to know this, if you decide to use it yourself. In Court, you may very well be asked to explain what it means, and if you say: *"It means I'm not prejudiced against anyone"*, they will know you don't know what you are talking about, and what you are really doing. So it's a very good idea to know exactly what it means, and exactly what it does, before employing this technique. Or, conversely, what it means if you receive a letter that says: *"Without Prejudice"*.

What it means is:

1. The Sender of the correspondence is reserving all Rights, and nothing in that correspondence should, or could, be taken to give up any Rights. (The things that are not being 'prejudiced' are one's Natural Inalienable Rights). It means that the Sender is openly stating: *"Not to be bound by any Contract unknowingly entered into, and only bound by those that meet the four criteria of Full Disclosure, Equal Considerations, Lawful Terms & Conditions, and Manifested Intent to Contract"*.

2. It - therefore - means that the correspondence **cannot** be entered into Court evidence **without the permission of the Creator**. So you can send anyone a letter, saying whatever you like. If you add: *"Without Prejudice"*, then that letter cannot be used against you in Court, unless you agree. (Obviously you can always submit your own correspondence into evidence ... that's always yours to submit if you choose ... you just can't submit theirs - if **either** side had written: *"Without Prejudice"*, see below).

3. And the same thing for them, of course. But there is more. Once either Party has used: *"Without Prejudice"*, **all further correspondence, from either side, in the current matter,** is protected by the original *"Without Prejudice"* - whether it is employed from then onwards (in further correspondence) or not.

So how does one use it, then?

Without Prejudice

Actually there is a very strong argument for not using it. If one is sure of one's position, and making strong, assertive, statements (which is the Freeman-on-the-Land way of writing), then one's Natural Inalienable Rights will be being asserted. And this needs no protection from any future Court case.

Quite the opposite, of course. Normally you would want what you said to the other Party to form a major part of your defence against them.

Thus, in that scenario, if you are sure of yourself (as you should be!) there is no point in using: *"Without Prejudice"*.

But then, there's nothing you can do to stop them using it. And then all your correspondence, from then onwards becomes, 'protected' (see (3), above) - as well as all theirs.

But this still does not alter the fact that you could submit your own correspondence into evidence and, if they chose to hide theirs, your statements would stand un-rebutted. Which would put you in a very powerful position.

[**Errata, August 2010, 2nd Edition:** It has been ascertained that correspondence containing *"Without Prejudice"* – from either Party to the communications - simply cannot be entered as evidence. Period. Therefore *"Without Prejudice"* should not be used, as was originally advised]

I suppose it's a bit like a game of Poker. But a Freeman-on-the-Land doesn't need to be bluffing, and therefore doesn't need to hide his or her cards - as long as they understand the game, and know what they are doing.

Chapter 25: Mass Mind Control & Enslavement

Previous Chapters have explained the triumvirate of the Grand Deception, namely *Money*, *Legalese* and *Religion*. And it is all fundamentally bound up with the illusion of 'money'.

Have you ever asked yourself: "*Where does money come from, in the first place?*"

You have? Well, congratulations! What was your answer?

I'll tell you what mine was. I decided that everything must have an ultimate source. My Common Sense told me that. I knew you could obtain money by working for some Company, as a salary or wages, and I knew you could also obtain money by selling things. I didn't think I was very far out on a limb with these thoughts.

But then I thought: "*Well, yes to all that ... but where did it come from originally?*"

Now most people would say: "*The Bank of England. The Royal Mint. They make it, don't they? Daft question, V!*"

So I thought: "*Well, is it such a daft question? I mean how do they put it into circulation? Do they hire a plane, and drop it from the sky? Well, I've never heard of that. Does someone stand with a bucketful of it, in Threadneedle Street, and throw it up in the air, for anyone to catch? Well, no, I've never heard of that either*".

I decided that there must by a 'system'. A mechanism. A **controlling** mechanism.

Am I bonkers? (Don't you **dare** answer that!)

Well, I decided that I wasn't quite ready for the Looney-Bin just yet. (Even though, by the way, I was actually born in one. In Sedgefield, in County Durham, during WWII. No, my mother wasn't mad. She had been evacuated to there. From out of London)

So I continued thinking. And I looked around. And I saw Banks. And I saw them going cap-in-hand for bailouts. And I saw some Banks and Building Societies going tits-up. And I thought: "*If they go belly up, then they can't be the source, because - if they were – going belly-up wouldn't happen*".

So I decided I didn't have the answer to my puzzle.

And I was left with a few serious (in my view) questions, which were:

1. How is 'money' created?

2. Who, or what, authorises it?
3. How is 'an amount of it' created?
4. How does it get into circulation?

I thought, for a moment, that I'd bitten off more than I could chew. But then I remembered what is supposed to be a Government Agency (but actually isn't!) called 'Her Majesty's Treasury'.

So I did a Freedom of Information Request to HM Treasury, asking them if they could kindly help me answer these questions.

And, to cut a long story short, they very kindly replied. And I have obtained four responses from them, which I include in an Appendix. The responses I obtained have been very helpful (in many ways), but not one has actually answered any of my four questions.

Well, you might suggest: *"That's probably because they don't know, Veronica!"*

And, I suppose, that is possible. But, if HM Treasury don't know, then who does? Does 'money' just appear by magic, then? (They say it doesn't grow on trees, but obviously that's where all the banknotes actually start their lives).

But here's another important facet. In one of the letters I sent to HM Treasury, I explained exactly what I understood the answers to my questions were. (Never ask a question unless you know the answer, otherwise you never know whether or not the answer you are given is bullshit). And I asked them to please confirm or deny my understanding. And, do you know what? They did not confirm - BUT DID NOT DENY - my understanding!

And denial would have been so easy. All they had to do was to say: *"No, sorry, but you are wrong"*. **But they didn't!**

You can check out the entire correspondence in the appropriate Appendix. You will see that HM Treasury did impart some very useful nuggets. Such as the fact that 'money' has not been backed by any precious metal since 1931. (In other words my lifetime, and probably yours).

And that currency is fiat, i.e. 'it has no intrinsic value'. And that the best you can ever do is to swap a tenner for two fivers, and so on. And that the issuance of 'money' (from wherever the ultimate source lies) is limited by Government Statute called The Currency Act.

Yes 'limited' ... but on who, which Authority, is this limitation placed? That's the question!

What were the answers I gave to HM Treasury, that they did not deny?

I asked the questions in this way:

1. What, precise, mechanism causes the release of 'some amount'? It must require some authority. Whose authority?

2. What defines 'the amount'?

3. How does this created money 'get into circulation'?

I self-answered those questions, back to HM Treasury, in this way:

Now we know the answer to (3) above is not that it is dropped from an airplane. Nor is it just because a Bank may up and demand it (otherwise Banks and Building Societies would not go out of business ... and what gives them a priority right to make such a demand, anyway?). (Although, of course, the recent bailouts were, precisely, 'because the Banks demanded it'. But this is very unusual, as I'm sure you will agree. Hence all the furore!)

If you want me to suggest answers for your consideration, answers that get to the heart of the matter, and may therefore explain to you what I consider to be the heart of the matter, then my considered understandings would be:

1. The precise mechanism for the creation of money is based on a Promissory Note, an IOU, signed by ANY individual when applying for a loan, mortgage, or equivalent. A 'promise to pay back'. (But, as you have already said, 'money is fiat, it has no value' ... so the 'pay back' is an empty promise ... just like the empty promise on a banknote itself)

2. The amount is the amount of the loan.

3. It is moved into circulation by making the amount available to whoever made the promise as a credit to an account on which s/he can draw upon.

Obviously, as you have explained, there are Statutory Limits placed on this mechanism, such that it doesn't run off into infinity. For example by raising Interest Rates such that the Promissory Notes generated by Loan Applications (1) become fewer.

HM Treasury did not deny these answers. They ignored them.

So what the hell does this mean?

It means that you apply for a loan of some kind. This could be a straight monetary loan, or a Credit Card, or a mortgage. Anything similar.

You make an application, by filling out an Application Form. You **think** it is an Application Form, asking the Loan Shark (commonly called a Bank, Bankster, Credit Company, Loan Company, Building Society ... you get the picture) to lend you some of their own money.

You think this because everyone else thinks the same thing. Even most of the Organic Robots who work for the Loan Sharks, processing applications, think that's what's happening.

But, it isn't.

When you sign the Loan Application, you are - in point of fact - **actually signing a cheque (a Bill of Exchange)**. A cheque drawn on an Account you did not realise you had. It is an Account that is automatically created, in the name of your *Legal Fiction Person*, when your birth was registered by your parents.

It is, fundamentally, a 'notional' Account. Really just numbers on a ledger (a computer database, these days).

The Account Number is somehow tied to your National Insurance Number and your Birth Certificate Number, and is named by taking your name in all capitals. Thus mine is VERONICA CHAPMAN, for example.

You send this cheque to the Loan Sharks, and they rub their hands in glee! Because you have made some 'money' for them! They then send this cheque to HM Treasury, or some Government Department 'known only to them'. (It is this knowledge, that is obviously sort-of secret that enables a Loan Shark to start up in business. My Freedom of Information Request was designed to extract that secret, but I was just stone-walled, because I'm not a Loan Shark. But notice ... my answers were not denied!)

The 'source of all money creation' will take the cheque and 'cash' it. 'Cashing it' comprises 'Authorising credit to the Bearer of the cheque'.

("I PROMISE TO PAY THE BEARER ON DEMAND ...", remember?)

So the Loan Shark is credited with the amount you signed for. If you applied for £50,000 then he is 'up' by £50,000!

Lovely jubbly! Clap hands ... walk away with your money (if he wanted to!). He could send you back a letter saying: *"Oh, sorry. Your Loan Application failed, after all!"*

And you would be none the wiser.

But he knows, if he always did that, people would stop applying for loans. Because there would be no point.

And he also knows if he moves that £50,000 into a Personal Account you can drawn on, then you will draw on it. And spend it. And you will think you have to pay it back (because everyone thinks that!), and you will also assume that you have to pay an additional amount called 'interest' (because everyone thinks that!)

And he knows that, in this latter situation, bearing in mind the way Compound Interest works, he is likely to end up with being paid TWICE (at the very least)!

Being paid twice for money you made!

Lovely, lovely, jubbly!

He steals something from you in the first place, and gets you to pay it back with Interest.

Oh boy! What are the words I'm looking for? I have a big problem finding the words, because fraud, theft, grand larceny just do not do the situation justice, in my humble opinion.

But that's not even where it ends. Oh yes ... there's lots more to come.

First of all, within that mechanism, even if it were not utterly fraudulent, there is only the mechanism for 'creating' the £50,000.

There is no mechanism at all for creating the Interest!

There is no mechanism for creating Interest. Which means that, under the current fraud, all loans could **never, ever, be paid off!** It is impossible! And that situation creates the dog-eat-dog so-called 'civilisation', which we all know only too well. Because we have to live in it, 24/7.

Only utter psychopaths, such as I described in the Chapter on the *Global Elite*, could have designed this, surely? You would need to be inhuman, surely?

But there is more.

Think about it.

You have a Government Agency 'creating money'. (It doesn't matter which one it is … it ain't you, that's for sure!). You have another Government Agency 'wanting money'. In the UK these two Agencies are HM Treasury and HM Revenue & Customs. In the united States this would be the US Treasury and the IRS.

Now, why can't HM Revenue & Customs, if they 'want money', get it directly from HM Treasury, who can 'make money'? 'Make as much money' as HM Revenue & Customs would ever need?

Mass Mind Control & Enslavement

Why bother you & I?

I can only think of one possible, plausible, reason: *'Money has to pass through us in order to keep our noses to the grindstone. In short, to keep us enslaved. It also has to pass through the Loan Sharks because the Global Elite own them, and that's how they obtain their massive wealth. And they own the Governments, thus they can ensure the legislation that enables these rip-offs. Generally without the knowledge of Joe Bloggs".*

To keep us in the prison-without-bars.

So now what is a bailout? Oh, it's pretty simple isn't it? And why there is so much angst involved. A bailout is the creation of money **without directly enslaving anyone to 'pay it back + interest'!** That's the reason for the angst.

But there is one more final thing to say. While the Loan Sharks are getting you & I to pay back – to them – the 'money' we, ourselves, created … **please note: They don't have any need (in turn) to pay it back to where they got it from … i.e. the Treasury.**

Oh lovely, lovely, lovely, lovely jubbly!!

Now, perhaps, you can understand why this Chapter was called *Mass Mind Control and Enslavement*?

I hope so. I've done my best to explain.

Why am I so convinced my answers are correct, and that this system operates the way I have explained? **Because there is no other way.** There is no other way to apply domination and mass mind-control over the entire planet. No other way such that even a dullard could not see through.

Every scrap of practical evidence we have supports this contention. Every prevarication we encounter universally supports this contention. Every media article is universally designed to hide this contention. Every book of Law, Accountancy, or Economics likewise. Every cognitive dissonance, from every Organic Robot, supports this contention. And our own Common Sense ***literally screams*** this contention.

Well, it does to me, at any rate.

Think about it. I have explained how *Money* & *Legalese* (supported by *Religions*) are massive illusions. Merely Belief Systems that could be jettisoned at the snap of finger and thumb. But, if that were the case, then domination and enslavement would no longer be possible.

On the other hand, the set-up of these Belief Systems was based on pandering to innate greed. It is very easy to see how the concept of 'money' could have been slipped into the universal psyche, based on: *"You worked hard for that, you should have some return"* and: *"This system is so much easier, more convenient, and more flexible than bartering. All we have to do is to set some standards".*

Constantly supported, at every turn, by psychologies whose design basis was 'greed' (Roman Empire - greed for domination? Feudal System - greed of the Nobility and the Monarchs?)

Never once did anyone (of importance) (apparently) say: *"I have to take, because I'm alive. But all I need is all I need. I don't need any more, thanks. It is dishonourable to take more than I need. I don't need to be greedy. I firmly believe we should all think that way. The only reward I will ever need is simply the honour of contributing selflessly to the good of one and all. And I think that should be the only reward anyone ever needs. Don't need 'money'. Don't need 'legal'. Don't need 'religion'. Don't need illusions!"*

Back in the relatively uncivilised days, when it all started, it is easy to see how people could be fooled. There was a time when they believed wholeheartedly in a God who made the Sun, and made it revolve around the (flat) Earth. And they never questioned these things. So why should they question 'the introduction of a Monetary System for their convenience'?

You would, and still do, need to take a step back and realise there is no dishonour in taking, and think about the Farmer, Miller, and Baker example, before it is possible to see the hoodwinking. You also have to understand the psychology of sicko psychopaths, who would actually want to create these illusions. You have to do this before the audacity of it ever has the slightest chance of dawning upon you.

And, even then, you would still need to answer why you even asked the question: *"What makes you so sure, Veronica, that your answers are right?"* The fact that this latter question even crosses your mind shows how ingrained the whole system of illusions has become.

You have to remember that we were made by sicko psychos, in the first place. The Annunaki (the Biblical Elohim/Nephilim). And their own half, of their creation, implanted the sickness of greed within us, so they knew exactly how to pander to it. We took our example from them. We knew no better. We copied their appalling example. We saw the way they behaved, and copied it, on the assumption that was the way to behave. We were told they were Gods - what chance did we actually have to know any better?

We can know better because of one thing. We are also half human. And, wherever 'human' came from, it came with compassion, conscience, empathy. It came with Common Sense. We have that, and they don't. We have a 'better nature', and they don't. That allows us to unravel their carefully constructed illusions, which I hope I have done in some small part.

Nevertheless the reality they have constructed, in order to maintain their domination, is immense and very, very, thorough.

But there is a way out. The *Examples* in this book show that. It comprises what is called Lawful Rebellion. It's a sort of 'lawful Judo', where you take the momentum of the attacker and use it against them, in your own defence, by adding dollops of Common Sense.

It is pointless telling me you have 'democracy' available to sort anything out, because your 'democracy' doesn't work. It doesn't work because those who attain the 'highest positions' all work for the same Masters (the Global Elite). It doesn't matter to the Global Elite whether the current Prime Minister is Tony B Liar, Gordon Brown, David Cameron (or whoever – at the time of writing), anymore than it makes any difference whether the US President is a DIMocrat or a RepuliCON.

The only thing anyone has at their disposal is not a useless 'democratic vote', but Lawful Rebellion - used to its most potent effect. **The vast majority of which can be done from your armchair, sitting in front of your computer, and writing letters in your own defence. The more people that do this, and stand up for themselves & their loved ones, the better.**

I'm sure you'll get the idea from these *Examples*. If not then you can join in the Forums that have been setup up at **forum.fmotl.com**.

The only reason why 'they' get away with any of this, is simple: **People just do not know their Rights.**

Rights that many of our forefathers gave their lives to protect.

It seems to me (at least) we need to do three things:

1. Learn or re-discover them;

2. Use them at all times;

3. Teach them to our children, so they never get lost or forgotten ever again.

Like them, you are a magnificent part of all that is, all that ever was, and all that ever will be. And it's long past time you claimed your freedom to be what you truly are. It's a lot more than just a seven-letter word.

Epilogue

Nothing I have written herein incites or induces violence of any kind. Nor any form of racial hatred. In point of fact, quite the contrary. All I've done is used Common Sense to point out the obvious, and documented methods by which perfectly peaceful, and perfectly lawful, rebellion can be achieved - entirely within the Law-of-the-Land.

And nowhere have I even suggested that anyone should break the Law-of-the-Land … or even Statutes for that matter. Once again, quite to the contrary.

And the Magna Carta 1215 says quite clearly, in Article 61, that it is the Inalienable Natural Right and Duty of each and every one of us to rebel with lawful excuse, as ever it may become necessary.

The content of this book indicates that such necessity is upon us, in my humble opinion.

I am fully prepared to go toe-to-toe with any Judge, Magistrate, Lawyer, Solicitor, Policyman, General, Admiral, Politician, King, Queen - indeed anyone - and stand on the Common Sense I have documented.

This is not a bluff.

I am not bluffing.

And I am not afraid of you.

Yes … you know who I mean. But, of course, you would never do that, would you?

Go toe-to-toe openly?

You would use your undoubted 'muscle', supplied by your meticulously-created Mind-Controlled Organic Robots, to lock me away without discussion. Or you would make sure I somehow disappeared. 'Character assassination'/'actual assassination' … you don't care … as long as the Truth remains covered up. 'Suicide' is your favourite one, of course. That and 'Strange accidents, when the CCTV just didn't happen to be working'.

You are snivelling, psychopathic cowards - and that's the way you act. That's the way you have to act. That's the way you've always acted, since the beginning of time. Because your actions could never withstand any scrutiny in the light of day. The 'hand' has to be kept 'hidden', doesn't it?

Epilogue

You disgust me, to the root of my soul. But do I hate you? No, not at all. I just want you locked up, away from decent people, to have a very long life – and the opportunity to consider all the evil and corruption you have perpetrated upon decent souls. I want to give you as long as possible to think about all that. In a real prison. With real bars. So there's no mistaking the situation: *"It's not corruption that's the problem. It's the* ***acceptance*** *of corruption that's the problem"* said Pat Rattigan in 2004.

And anyone who reads this book will know what you are. If anything happens to me, as it has done to others who have revealed Truths, then what I have said becomes Truth anyway.

But then left to stand as it is, the blinding obviousness of what I've written is, frankly, rather hard to rebut, is it not?

Bit of a problem, then.

And you do, after all, have an awful lot to lose.

But, for me: *"Freedom's just another word for nothing left to lose"*, as Kris Kristofferson once wrote.

Sue me. Prove you are not a psychopath. Let's have your DNA examined by a Court … even a de facto one.

You have no clothes! You Emperors have no clothes! The bits of blue cloth you wear, with metallic trinkets attached, the wigs you don, the trappings & robes you wear … still leave you as naked as the day that you were born!

(If I ever say anything different, 'it will be the drugs talking'. The ones your Robots will have used, without my permission or my consent).

Appendix A: Templates & Usage Disclaimer

Disclaimer: *You are playing with fire. And you know what happens if you do that, without knowing exactly what you are doing. It is, therefore, absolutely essential that you have read this book from end to end before attempting to rebut any legal action taken against you. And, furthermore, you do it in accordance with the information herein entirely at your own risk. The techniques explained herein will not, necessarily work in any case if you have already been through Court Proceedings because, at that point, you will have tacitly agreed to be the Legal Fiction Person.*

All the information contained in this book is used entirely at your own discretion. In no way should anything be read herein other than to encourage you to consider possibilities. And to use your Common Sense to understand the deceptive world in which you live. There is no encouragement or incitement to take any actions of any kind.

The Templates can be found on the Internet, on the links given below. This is the best way to present them, because of their 'dynamic' nature. They can be used for more than one circumstance, for example if more than one Legal Fiction Person is involved i.e. '**Mr. & Mrs.**'. Furthermore certain prefixing can be invoked - depending on circumstances

The responses to them will either be 'standard' - generally to repeat Statutes in return (fundamentally they have no idea what you are talking about, and respond by rote).

Where necessary the Templates include the condition of '**estoppel by acquiescence**', and so this should be pointed out in the reply, specifically:

(a) No response to the Human Self has been forthcoming (response was still addressed to Legal Fiction Person), and this is the last time you will reply pointing this out;

(b) No response in substance has been forthcoming;

(c) Thus '**permanent and irrevocable lawful estoppel by acquiescence**' has been gained, due to their dishonour;

(d) Your original Conditional Agreement removed all Controversy, and thus removed the possibility of Court Action on their part;

(e) Notice that henceforth a charge of £500 will be levied for letters sent that appertain to the matter in hand (where a communication is addressed to your Human Self). Correspondence continued to be addressed to your Legal Fiction Person will be returned unopened, marked: ***"No Legal Fictions dwell here. Only Human Beings. Try La-La Land"***;

These things tend to tie them up on knots. If they still persist, let them. You've already won, so why should you care what they do? You can write back and tell them that you've already won so, whatever they do – they've already lost. Point out that, if they go to Court, their case will be dismissed, and that you will make a Counterclaim for harassment in the sum of £50,000 for all the UNLAWFUL stress you have suffered. (Make sure you always do this from what you are commonly called, and not the Legal Fiction Name they addressed, "Without Prejudice", etc. The Templates make sure of all this). The best thing is not to open letters addressed to your Legal Fiction Person, but to return them unopened, as explained above. Phone calls: Don't admit to your name, and DO NOT quote the "first line of your address". **Give them absolutely nothing (not even the time of day, if possible).**

Have I actually done this myself? Yes. On a number of occasions. What happened to me? Nothing ... as yet. Except the chance to write this book.

It is felt that the Templates should be self-explanatory.

I have been asked: *"Which template do I use:?".* The answer to that is: *"The templates are the 2nd Phase. The 1st Phase is to stop paying. You will then receive a letter, which you will need to rebut. You will then know which Rebuttal Template to use".*

The only Templates presented herein are those that have been proven to work. However, while they start the 'rebuttal ball rolling', they do not - necessarily - stop the process immediately. It is often necessary to follow up, explaining the difference between 'legal' and 'lawful' (**their** response will always be in the 'legal sense'), and pointing out that the 'lack of response in substance' has gained the estoppel, explained above.

Type **templates.fmotl.com** into your Browser to obtain personalised rebuttal letters for the following situations:

Debt Collection Agency Rebuttal.

This Template is available in dynamic form via **templates.fmotl.com**. Below is a generalised sample, where ?N? are numbers to be replaced by the following:

?1? = Your Address Line 1
?2? = Your Address Line 2
?3? = Your Address Line 3
?4? = Your Address Line 4
?5? = Your Address Line 5
?6? = Your Address Line 6
?7? = Your PostCode
?8? = Your Letter Date
?9? = DCA Reference Number
?10? = DCA Reference Date
?11? = DCA Address Line 1
?12? = DCA Address Line 2
?13? = DCA Address Line 3
?14? = DCA Address Line 4
?15? = DCA Address Line 5
?16? = DCA Address Line 6
?17? = Your Given Name
?18? = Your Family Name

DO NOT SIGN IT. There is no need. 'They' often do not sign anything written to you, so why give them a Signature to forge? Send it 'registered'.

In care of:
?1?
?2?
?3?
?4?
?5?
?6?
Near: [?7?]

?8?

Re: ?9?, dated ?10?.

Notice of Request To Cease Harrassment.

To:
?11?
?12?
?13?
?14?
?15?
?16?

Dear Sirs,

Please read the following notice thoroughly and carefully before responding. It is a notice. It informs you. It means what it says.

I refer to your letter dated ?10?.

As you are a third party intervener in this matter acting without authority, I DO NOT give you permission to interfere in my commercial affairs as you have no legal standing. I do not have a contract with you and any permission that you believe you may have from me is hereby withdrawn. If you believe that you have power of attorney to act on my behalf you are hereby fired, and any consent that you believe you may have, tacit or otherwise, is hereby withdrawn.

I am familiar with the terms of Section 40 of the Administration of Justice Act 1970, and the Protection from Harassment Act 1997. And I believe, should you continue in contacting me after my request for you to cease your activity, that you will be guilty of harassment and blackmail, and you will be in breach of these acts, and you will be reported to the relevant bodies.

I am well aware of Section 40, sub-section (3) which you may consider entitles you to proceed. However upon full commercial liability and penalty of perjury you will need to supply the following Proofs of Claims:

1. Proof of Claim that your actions are reasonable.

2. Proof of Claim that any obligation on my part is due, or believed by you to be due to you, and not to some other party.

3a. Proof of Claim that any obligation on my part is to yourself by providing sight of the appropriate contract, or

3b. Proof of Claim that any obligation on my part to persons for whom you act by providing sight of the appropriate contract.

4. Proof of Claim that any obligation on my part protects you from any future loss.

5. Proof of Claim that any obligation on my part is enforcement of a legal process on a Human Being under Common Law jurisdiction, who cannot possibly have such liability under said jurisdiction.

You would of course need to provide these Proofs, including showing the full and audited accounting, if you chose to go to law.

Please also note that if you contact me by telephone, after a formal request not to, you will also be in breach of the Wireless Telegraphy Act (1949) and, as such, I will report you to both Trading Standards and The Office of Fair Trading. And take further note that continued telephone calls after the receipt of a request not to call may constitute a criminal offence under Section 127 of the Communications Act 2003.

Finally, you do not, nor have you ever had, my permission to use or process my personal data in any way, and so pursuant to the Data Protection Act 1998, I hereby demand that you cease use of any and all data with regard to me, and that you immediately destroy all of my data held on your records. Failure to do so will result in a report being submitted to The Information Commissioner for Data Protection breaches.

You will be deemed to have been served notice of my request and I will deem it served three (3) days from the date of this letter. This has been sent by recorded delivery. I am advising you that any communications from you including but not limited to letters, phone calls and text messages received after this date will be recorded/noted with the intention of them being used as evidence.

Do not contact me again.

Sincerely and without ill will, vexation or frivolity,

?17?: of the ?18? family

Templates & Usage Disclaimer

WITHOUT PREJUDICE, i.e. all Natural Inalienable Rights Reserved

Please address all future correspondence in the matter to a direct Human Self, namely ?17?: of the ?18? family, as commonly called.

Encl: Original paperwork as received.

Charge or Demand Rebuttal (incl. Fixed Penalty Notices).

This Template is available in dynamic form via **templates.fmotl.com**. Below is a generalised sample, where ?N? are numbers to be replaced by the following:

?1? = Your Address Line 1
?2? = Your Address Line 2
?3? = Your Address Line 3
?4? = Your Address Line 4
?5? = Your Address Line 5
?6? = Your Address Line 6
?7? = Your PostCode
?8? = Your Letter Date
?9? = Charge/Demand Reference Number
?10? = Charge/Demand Reference Date
?11? = Charge/Demand Address Line 1
?12? = Charge/Demand Address Line 2
?13? = Charge/Demand Address Line 3
?14? = Charge/Demand Address Line 4
?15? = Charge/Demand Address Line 5
?16? = Charge/Demand Address Line 6
?17? = Your Given Name
?18? = Your Family Name
?19? = The Legal Fiction Name, **exactly as printed in the Demand**.
?20? = The Amount Demanded

This has been organised for a Fixed Penalty Charge. This same (or similar) wording could be used for any Demand in general.

DO NOT SIGN IT. There is no need. 'They' often do not sign anything written to you, so why give them a Signature to forge? <u>Send it 'registered'.</u>

In care of:
?1?
?2?
?3?
?4?
?5?
?6?
Near: [?7?]

?8?

Re: ?9?, dated ?10?.

Notice of Discharge of Outstanding Fixed Penalty Charge and Request for Clarification.

?11?
?12?
?13?
?14?
?15?
?16?

Dear Sirs,

Please read the following notice thoroughly and carefully before responding. It is a notice. It informs you. It means what it says.

The reason why you need to read carefully is simple. I am offering conditional agreement. This removes controversy, and means that you no longer have any ultimate recourse to a court of law in this matter, because there is no controversy upon which it could adjudicate. You always have the option of dragging these conditions into a court of law only to be told that they are, indeed, perfectly lawful. That is, of course, always your prerogative should you decide to waste your time.

For this reason it is important that you consider and respond to the offer in substance. The 'nearest official form' will not suffice, and consequently is likely to be ignored by myself without any dishonour on my part.

On the other hand there is a time-limit on the agreement being offered. It is reasonable, and if it runs out then you and all associated parties are in default, removing any and all lawful excuse on your part for proceeding in this matter.

For these reasons it is recommended that you carefully consider this notice and respond in substance, which means actually addressing the points raised herein.

You have apparently made allegations of unacceptable conduct on my part.

You have apparently made demands upon me.

I do not understand those apparent demands and therefore cannot lawfully fulfill them. I seek clarification of your document so that I may act according to the law and maintain my entire body of inalienable Natural Rights.

Failure to accept this offer to clarify and to do so completely and in good faith within 7 (seven) days will be deemed by all parties to mean you and your principal or other parties abandon all demands upon me.

I conditionally accept your offer to agree that I am legal fiction 'person' ?19? and that I owe £?20? for services rendered by your company, upon proof of claim of all of the following:

1. Upon proof of claim that I am a person, and not a human being.

2. Upon proof of claim that you know what a 'person' actually is, in legal terms.

3. Upon proof of claim that you know the difference between a 'human being' and a 'person', legally speaking.

4. Upon proof of claim that you know the difference between 'legal' and a 'lawful'.

5. Upon proof of claim that I am legal fiction 'person' ?19?, being the entity to which your paperwork was addressed, and not ?17?: of the ?18? family, as commonly called.

6. Upon proof of claim that the charge was the result of a lawful investigation unmarred by prejudice.

7. Upon proof of claim that I am a member of the society whose statutes and subsisting regulations you are enforcing.

8. Upon proof of claim that I showed you some sort of identification.

9 Upon proof of claim that there is a nameable society that I belong to and that the laws covered within any alleged transgressions state that they apply to me within that named society.

Sincerely and without ill will, vexation or frivolity,

?17?: of the ?18? family

WITHOUT PREJUDICE, i.e. all Natural Inalienable Rights Reserved

Templates & Usage Disclaimer

Please address all future correspondence in the matter to a direct Human Self, namely ?17?: of the ?18? family, as commonly called.

Encl: Original paperwork as received.

Court de facto Summons Rebuttal.

This Template is available in dynamic form via **templates.fmotl.com**. Below is a generalised sample, where ?N? are numbers to be replaced by the following:

?1? = Your Address Line 1
?2? = Your Address Line 2
?3? = Your Address Line 3
?4? = Your Address Line 4
?5? = Your Address Line 5
?6? = Your Address Line 6
?7? = Your PostCode
?8? = Your Letter Date
?9? = Summons Reference Number
?10? = Summons Reference Date
?11? = Court Name/Address Line 1
?12? = Court Address Line 2
?13? = Court Address Line 3
?14? = Court Address Line 4
?15? = Court Address Line 5
?16? = Court Address Line 6
?17? = Your Given Name
?18? = Your Family Name
?19? = The Legal Fiction Name, **exactly as printed in the Summons.**

DO NOT SIGN IT. There is no need. 'They' often do not sign anything written to you, so why give them a Signature to forge? Send it 'registered'.

Templates & Usage Disclaimer

In care of:
?1?
?2?
?3?
?4?
?5?
?6?
Near: [?7?]

?8?

Re: ?9?, dated ?10?.

Notice of Request for Clarification of Paperwork Received.

To:
The Clerk of the Court
?11?
?12?
?13?
?14?
?15?
?16?

Dear Sirs,

The enclosed paperwork was delivered to the address at which I dwell.

It was addressed in the name ?19?.

I have been led to believe this signifies that the paperwork was addressed to a legal fiction known as a PERSON, which is, in point of fact, the name of some CORPORATION.

I would be most grateful if you would kindly confirm or deny my understanding in this respect.

As a sovereign Human Being, with a living soul, and consequently (as I understand it) under Common Law jurisdiction (i.e. the law-of-the-land, as opposed to Corporate or Statute Law, namely the law-of-the-sea), I am not entirely sure why I have received this paperwork, and would be grateful for any clarification in this matter. I have no wish to dishonour any valid and lawful obligation on my part.

Article 45 of the Magna Carta 1215 states quite clearly: ***"We will appoint as justices, constables, sheriffs, or bailiffs only those who know the law of the realm and who wish to observe it well"***, and this cannot be repealed or voided in any way because it pre-dates all Parliaments, and furthermore the document itself says so in other Articles.

And said document bears the Royal Seal. In consequence of this I assume you can clarify, in lay terms, the points raised herein.

According to Dun & Bradstreet there is a registered company known as ?11?. Since it is possible to obtain a D&B Credit Report on said company, it seems reasonable to assume that it is in business, actively trading, and offering services. Please confirm that your good selves have no connection with said Trading Company, and that said paperwork was not an issuance from it, being merely an offer to provide a service.

Sincerely and without ill will, vexation or frivolity,

?17?: of the ?18? family

WITHOUT PREJUDICE, i.e. all Natural Inalienable Rights Reserved

Please address all future correspondence in the matter to a direct Human Self, namely ?17?: of the ?18? family, as commonly called.

Encl: Original paperwork as received.

Appendix B: Freedom of Information interactions with HM Treasury

There is a Website that provides for UK Freedom of Information Requests, called *WhatDoTheyKnow.com*. I made the following Freedom of Information Request to HM Treasury on 3rd February, 2009:

> ***Dear Sir or Madam,***
>
> ***Under the Freedom of Information Act I would like an answer to the following question:***
>
> ***How, precisely, is money created?***
>
> ***For your information I have been given to understand that it is created by means of Promissory Notes. In more detail, when a human being signs a 'promise to pay' (known colloquially as an IOU), which can stand until the end of time. And that the human being's signature on that promise renders said promise lawful.***
>
> ***Can you please be so kind as to confirm or deny my understanding and, if necessary, correct my understanding?***
>
> ***Thank you.***
>
> ***Yours faithfully, ... etc.***

I was told that they did not need to answer such questions under the Freedom of Information Act. That they were only required to pull numbers from their databases, in response to requests for such numbers. However, as a kindness to me, they would respond as they were able.

A copy of their response is Figures B1 & B2.

Paul Morran had not answered my question, but did supply, in Paragraph 7, sentence 2, the answer: "*You are correct in essence that this amounts to an IOU*". And there were some nuggets of information in Paragraph 5, for example, sentence 3: "*Modern 'currency' is known as 'fiat' money; it is artificially created, has no value in itself ...*".

Figure B1: First response from HM Treasury (1st Page).

HM TREASURY

1 Horse Guards Road London SW1A 2HQ

Information Rights Unit

Tel: 0207 270 4558
Fax: 0207 270 4861

www.hm-treasury.gov.uk
public.enquiries@hm-treasury.gsi.gov.uk

Ref: 9/96

Veronica Chapman

By email: request-7551-d437f2a6@whatdotheyknow.com

26 February 2009

Dear Ms Chapman

Freedom of Information Act 2000: 'Money'

Thank you for your enquiry dated 3 February requesting information under the Freedom of Information Act 2000. I have also taken account of the follow-up email sent on 10 February; this does not seem to change the substance of your request, but does provide some insight to the intent of what is otherwise a very broad question.

2. You asked –

> *how precisely is money created?*
>
> *For your information I have been given to understand that it is created by means of Promissory notes. In more detail, when a human being signs a 'promise to pay' (known colloquially as an IOU) which can stand until the end of time. And that the human being's signature on that promise renders said promise lawful.*
>
> *Can you please be so kind as to confirm or deny my understanding and, if necessary, correct my understanding?*

3. I need to point out that the purpose of the Act is to oblige authorities to disclose recorded information. Broad questions and requests for explanation or confirmation of a view, as in your enquiry, are not valid requests under the Act. The information Commissioner has published a 'Charter for Responsible Requesters', which includes guidance about how to formulate a request for the best prospects of success. I enclose a copy with this reply.

4. To be helpful, I offer the following comments, although your question is really an academic one and HM Treasury is not perhaps best placed to answer it.

5. Money is whatever is accepted in a society as payment for goods and services, or for repayment of debts. Gold is a form of what is called 'commodity money', not created, but perceived as having value in itself. Modern 'currency' is known as 'fiat money': it is artificially created, has no value in itself and the basis for its use in exchange is typically a government edict. Since its foundation in 1694, the Bank of England has issued notes promising to pay the bearer a sum of money. The promise

Figure B2: First response from HM Treasury (2nd Page).

could be made good by the Bank paying out gold in exchange for its notes. The link with gold helped to maintain the value of the notes, although the link was sometimes suspended, for example, in wartime. The link with gold was fully broken in 1931 and since that time there has been no other asset into which holders have the right to convert Bank of England notes. Members of the public may only exchange notes for other Bank of England notes. This is set out Section 1(4) of the Currency and Bank Notes Act 1954 Act: "the holder of [Bank of England] bank notes of any denominations shall be entitled, on a demand made by him during office hours at the head office of the Bank of England or, in the case of notes payable also at some place other than the head office, either at the head office or at that other place, to receive in exchange for the notes bank notes of such lower denominations, being bank notes which for the time being are legal tender in the United Kingdom or in England and Wales, as he may specify."

6. The Bank of England is required to back all banknotes issued with securities (such as Government bonds), which are held by the Issue Department. Public faith in the pound is fostered through the Bank of England's operation of monetary policy, the statutory object of which is price stability. Monetary stability is the first of the Bank's core purposes.

7. The judicial citation you provided seemed to be concerned with the category of 'credit money'. You are correct that in essence this amounts to an IOU. Indeed banknotes that 'promise to pay the bearer on demand' are essentially credit money, as are government gilts and other financial instruments. It is arguable that all money is ultimately credit money, to which the only alternative is barter of goods and services - with attendant disadvantages! The second of the Bank of England's core purposes - financial stability – is concerned with maintaining confidence in the credit money in terms of the financial system as a whole. The Bank works with HM Treasury and the Financial Services Authority to promote confidence in the UK financial system. But financial markets are now so global in reach that stability depends on international cooperation and standards.

8. None of the above suggests to us that mortgages contracted with financial institutions that have subsequently been undermined by the credit crunch would be judged void – if that was the suggestion from your reference. But, just as HM Treasury is not set up for academic purposes, neither are we in a position to offer legal advice.

9. I hope this is helpful. If you have any queries about this letter, please contact me. It will be helpful to us if you remember to quote the reference number above in any future communications.

Paul Morran
Information Rights Unit

Rather than bog up the Freedom of Information website, I decided to take Paul Morran up on this offer to contact him further. So I sent the following e-mail:

> *Dear Sirs,*
>
> *I recently submitted a Freedom of Information request that can be read via this link: http://www.whatdotheyknow.com/request/the_creation_of_money*
>
> *It was responded to very courteously by your colleague Mr. Paul Morran.*
>
> *However the fundamental question was only answered by default. Nevertheless that default answer is now the law-of-the-land, in other words now becomes a part of established Common Law.*
>
> *Based on that situation, and under Common Law courtesy, I am now writing to you for further - more detailed - answers in the form of specific clarifications.*
>
> *Please remain assured that I do not wish to 'pull rank'. That is, by being a Member of the Public. A Human Being who, by virtue of my supreme and absolute power, colludes with others of the same rank to provide your ultimate authorisation for existence as 'HM Treasury'.*
>
> *You may consider that your authorisation derives from empowerment by Government Statute. That is fair enough, but who empowers the Government? The Queen? Wrong answer, because who empowers the Queen?*
>
> *There is only one answer. Those with the power to do that. Which is us, the Human Beings who populate this Country of ours.*
>
> *We empower the Queen via the Coronation Oath. We empower the Government by elections.*
>
> *You cannot give someone, or even some 'body' (such as a group of representatives), more than you, yourself, possess. Consequently no-one can empower either the Monarch, or the Government (or HM Treasury) with more power than they, themselves, possess.*
>
> *All this is just saying one thing: If I ask a question with due courtesy, I have the inalienable Right to have it answered courteously, IN FULL, on pain of perjury and full*

commercial liability, and IN TRUTH (as far as is practicable).

You have extended Common Law courtesy until now. And I have responded as courteously as was (I think) possible. And I sincerely hope that will continue.

So now I ask you ('money' is henceforth in quotes as defined by Mr. Morran in his original answer):

1) Who authorises the creation of 'money'? Upon whose signature (or signatures) is it created? 2) For what reason is AN AMOUNT created? 3) Do you hold a Live Birth Trust (or some such) for each individual who is alive? If so, is the Reference Number the same as a National Insurance Number, and is any such account 'named' to the legal fiction PERSON of that individual? And, furthermore, if this is the case, is the associated Human Being Prime Creditor on the account?

There may be more questions, depending on your truthful answers, which I trust can be responded to within a matter of a few days at the very most.

If there is any reason why you cannot give answers, then please be so kind as to direct me to a source of them.

I thank you in anticipation,

Sincerely, without ill-will, frivolity or vexation,

Veronica: of the Chapman family as commonly called, a live Human being with a living soul. "Veronica: Chapman", for short (there is no "Ms.", "Miss" or "Mrs.", because those are legal fiction PERSONS and not my Human Self. Only my Human Self has (a) a Mind with which to devise these questions and interpret/comprehend the answers and (b) Eyes with which to read the answers)

And I received back the letter shown in Figures B3 & B4.

I analysed this response as follows:

My requests seem to find their way back to Paul: of the Morran family. He is turning into being one of my favourite people of all time.

Notice he addresses me as Veronica: of the Chapman family! But what does his response mean?

Figure B3: Second response for HM Treasury (1st Page).

HM TREASURY

1 Horse Guards Road London SW1A 2HQ

Information Rights Unit

Tel: 0207 270 4558
Fax: 0207 270 4861

www.hm-treasury.gov.uk
public.enquiries@hm-treasury.gsi.gov.uk

Veronica Chapman

By email: [redacted]

Ref: 9/200

30 March 2009

Dear Veronica of the Chapman family

Freedom of Information Act 2000: 'Money'

Your latest enquiry dated 3 March has found its way back to me. I am treating your numbered questions as requests for information under the Freedom of Information Act.

2. You asked –

   i. *Who authorises the creation of money?*

   ii. *For what reason is AN AMOUNT created?*

   iii. *Do you hold a Live Birth Trust (or some such) for each individual who is alive? If so, is the Reference Number the same as a National Insurance Number, and is any such account 'named' to the legal fiction PERSON of that individual? And, furthermore, if this is the case, is the associated Human Being prime Creditor on the account?*

3. Our previous replies have directed you to Bank of England resources that address the question of money on a broader interpretation. You have complained that my previous answers did not directly address your concerns. In the light of your commentary on previous requests at 'WhatDoTheyKnow.com', I am interpreting the first two parts of your present request to mean who authorises the issue of UK currency and for what reason is new currency issued.

   i. The Bank of England authorises the issue of bank notes; the Royal Mint authorises the issue of coinage. Both exercise their authority under remit from HM Treasury and under statute. The statutory framework is set by the Currency Act 1983, available here –

      http://www.opsi.gov.uk/RevisedStatutes/Acts/ukpga/1983/cukpga_19830009_en_1

   ii. Currency is issued in response to demand; if demand exceeded availability, users would be constrained to make greater use of cheques and electronic transfers. Statistics on banknotes in circulation are available here –

      http://www.bankofengland.co.uk/banknotes/about/stats.htm#1

Figure B4: Second response from HM Treasury (2nd Page).

4. We do not hold information relevant to your third question, as far as we can determine. A search of our electronic records does not identify any documents containing the term "Live Birth Trust Fund" or "Live Birth Trust" and these terms have not been recognised by officials we have consulted therefore we can only guess at what you might mean by it. To be helpful, I can say that the system of National Insurance Numbers is primarily used simply to record National Insurance contributions against individuals, which determine their entitlement to certain state benefits – as explained at the Directgov web page below. There is no government system that keeps account of individuals as creditors.

http://www.direct.gov.uk/en/MoneyTaxAndBenefits/Taxes/BeginnersGuideToTax/DG_4015904

5. I hope this is helpful. If you have any queries about this letter, please contact me. It will be helpful to us if you remember to quote the reference number above in any future communications.

Well, first of all we are being directed to the Currency Act 1983. At the time of writing I have not looked at this, but certainly will. **(Now been looked at ... see below)**

More importantly, in my view, we now have it in writing that: *"currency is issued in response to demand"*.

And: *"If demand exceeded availability, users would be constrained to make greater use of cheques and electronic transfers"*. Very curious way of saying something? Because what, exactly, is it actually saying?

Finally Paul: Morran goes on to deny the existence of Live Birth Trusts, and any connection with one's National Insurance Number.

[**Errata, August 2010, 2nd Edition:** It has been pointed out that Paul Morran did not actually or specifically deny the existence of Live Birth Trusts, and therefore my apologies for what was written above. In the interim, however - since writing the 1st Edition - we have come to the conclusion - in the light of experience - that (a) very few, if any, know or would know the real truth, and (b) that it probably doesn't matter anyway since - ultimately - it just means 'money' does not exist. And Paul Morran implied that in his first response, if one reads between his lines]

An interesting response, all told, but it begs so many questions:

1. ***"currency is issued in response to demand"***? Whose demand? Maybe this is covered in the Currency Act?

2. ***"If demand exceeded availability, users would be constrained to make greater use of cheques and electronic transfers"***. If demand exceeded availability? Whose demand ... see above. **'Availability'** ... whaaaaat? Paul has already told us that: '*money has no value*'. **'The availability of something without value'** means what? 'Money' is nothing more than **an idea, a belief. The availability of beliefs is infinite**.

3. **'users'**? Is that us? I assume so. But that is not, necessarily the case. It could easily mean just Banks, Building Societies, etc. Those who directly interface with HM Treasury. I'm not sure what this means.

4. And: ***"these users would be constrained to make greater use of cheques and electronic transfers"***? To do what? To pass 'money' around, but what money? Where is it coming from (to be passed around under constraints)?

All in all, this seems to be totally circular. Well, almost. I think progress is being made, slowly but surely.

Freedom of Information interactions with HM Treasury

I can't see how anything here actually contradicts anything else I've said, except that we are having Live Birth Trusts dismissed. I find the latter so hard to believe. Accounting and bookkeeping practices absolutely scream some kind of mechanism like that, tied to the National Insurance Number. They could not possibly run a free-for-all system. It is against the ingrained robotic nature of any Accountant. **Accounts must add up**. Otherwise Accountants have no 'profession' to speak of.

And why, in that case, is our National Insurance Number demanded left, right, centre, on **all** 'official paperwork', and a considerable amount of 'private', or 'non-official', paperwork?

And, subsequently, after reading most of the Currency Act:

This just seems to deal with the standards for minting, etc.

(As if it makes any difference to a Belief System. An Idea. An Illusion)

Notice ... there it is again: **'bank notes' means notes of the Bank payable to bearer on demand**. Totally circular. Chasing the roots of 'money' will have you running round in circles. You might as well chase rainbows or unicorns, which is the same thing. Everyone would get the actual idea if the banknote said: *"I promise to pay the Bearer on demand 5 unicorns"*. Which would be just as true as what it actually says.

However there was one bit I laughed at: *"(2) For the purposes of this section, the limit is £13,500 million or such other amount as may from time to time be specified in a direction given by the Treasury."*

Yea ... tell that to Gordon Brown.

So. No. We still don't know the answers to the questions I asked. These are:

1. How is 'money' created? (How is the belief manifested in the form of Tokens?) 2. For what reason is 'an amount' created? 3. Who looks at that reason, decides it is valid, and therefore authorises the creation of 'an amount'? 4. How is 'an amount that has been created passed into circulation'? Who is it passed to, and why?

And the answers are contained within this book. **Because there is no other way.**

Why am I so concerned about this? Is it because I want buckets of it?

Actually no, that's not the reason at all. I would like to see us get rid of it once and for all.

The reason I'm so concerned is because **I don't like having the michael taken out of me**. That's the reason. And I don't see why the michael should be taken out of everyone else, either. That's the reason.

And I don't see why people of all shapes, sizes and ages should be bombed, shot, maimed, killed, tortured, put through excruciating agonies, enslaved in the most draconian manner ... all based on a mickey-take. That's the main reason.

So I sent another e-mail. This is what I said:

PLEASE FORWARD THIS E-MAIL (AS NECESSARY) TO YOUR COLLEAGUE PAUL: MORRAN

Dear Paul: of the Morran family,

I cannot thank you enough for the responses you have already made. I don't know whether or not you are irritated by my persistence. I hope not, because the questions I've asked affect yourself, your family, your friends, and everyone else.

I fully appreciate that you have strived manfully to answer the questions I have raised in the past.

But we still have not got to the heart of the matter.

Thank you for the reference to the Currency Act 1983, but - by my reading - that only defines the standards for coinage and banknotes such as to be acceptable legal tender, and does not really answer my questions.

May we please start again?

May I please ask you the following question?

"Is HM Treasury the SOLE authority that regulates the issuance of 'an amount' INTO CIRCULATION at any point in time?" (This does not mean the production of coins and/or banknotes that represent 'money'. You have already answered that as the Royal Mint and the Bank of England, respectively)

What I'm trying to get to is: Who tells the Royal Mint to issue a certain number of coins? Who tells the Bank of England to issue a certain number of banknotes? Who ... if not HM Treasury?

Best + thanking you in anticipation + apologies if you find this irritating,

Veronica: of the Chapman family.

The response I received is Figures B5 & B6.

Figure B5: Third response for HM Treasury (1st Page).

HM TREASURY

1 Horse Guards Road London SW1A 2HQ

Information Rights Unit

Tel: 0207 270 4558
Fax: 0207 270 4861

Veronica: of the Chapman family

www.hm-treasury.gov.uk
public.enquiries@hm-treasury.gsi.gov.uk

By email: [redacted]

Ref: 9/274

6 April 2009

Dear Veronica

Freedom of Information Act 2000: Money

Thank you for your enquiry dated 30 March. I am treating your request under the Freedom of Information Act 2000.

2 You asked for the following information –

> *Is HM Treasury the SOLE authority that regulates the issuance of 'an amount' INTO CIRCULATION at any point in time. What I am trying to get to is: who tells the Royal Mint to issue a certain number of coins; who tells the Bank of England to issue a certain number of banknotes; who ... if not HM Treasury?*

3 In passing, you noted that the Currency Act 1983 we previously referred you to, seemed only to define standards for coinage and banknotes. In fact it does more. Section 2 provides a check on the amount of currency in circulation. Within an approved ceiling, the Bank has executive responsibility for maintaining the level of notes in circulation. Treasury approval is required if the Bank sees justification for raising the ceiling. Subject to the constraints set out in the Act, such increases may have to be submitted to Parliament. (Coinage typically accounts for less than 10% of currency in circulation and supply is managed by the Royal Mint, on behalf of the Treasury and in consultation with APACS, the UK payments association.)

4. It may be helpful to highlight that the government now relies on controlling inflation, rather than merely controlling notes and coin in circulation, to achieve monetary policy goals. The Bank's Monetary Policy Committee is responsible for setting Central Bank interest rates in order to achieve the inflation target, and for open reporting to the Chancellor where there is significant divergence from target. In exceptional circumstances, such as the present, the Bank needs the Chancellor's authorisation for extraordinary measures such as quantitative easing. Monetary policy key documents are available on Treasury website at the following link -

http://www.hm-treasury.gov.uk/ukecon_mon_index.htm

Figure B6: Third response from HM Treasury (2nd Page).

5. You questioned whether I was irritated by your persistence. Personally speaking, I am intrigued rather than irritated. I confess I am slightly frustrated when you say 'we still have not got to the heart of the matter', because I do not understand what the heart of the matter is, for you, in this context. However, the Act does not oblige you to provide such assistance.

6. Speaking for Treasury, we do need to have regard to the resources that a prolonged exchange could absorb. If your requests continue in the same vein and it becomes plain that repeated requests are bringing us no closer to identifying information that answers your wishes, we might need to bring matters to a close by invoking section 14; I enclose a copy of the relevant guidance from the Information Commissioner. Of course, we would much rather be able to provide information you want.

I decided it was time to pull out all the stops, so I sent the following e-mail:

Dear Paul,

Thank you once again for your kind response.

You say, in (5) you are disappointed at my statement about 'not yet having got to the heart of the matter' and that you have to consider the resources available to answer me. I understand that, of course. However I do write on behalf of not just myself. All the information you have provided is valuable, in my humble opinion. And many others are watching this correspondence which is - after all - public information, of course.

I would say that your answers have, actually, moved the situation a little closer to the heart of the matter each time, and some progress has been made.

OK. Well, in (5) you say that you do not understand what the heart of the matter is for me. May I then please try to explain, as far as I am able?

The heart of the matter, what I'm trying to get to, was actually in my very first FoI question.

And I suggested an answer, and requested confirmation or denial.

I suggested that money was created on the basis of Promissory Notes. And, in your first response, you said that this was true "in essence". But you did not say it was true "in fact". Which is different.

So, the heart of the matter is this:

1. What, precise, mechanism causes the release of 'some amount'? It must require some authority. Whose authority?

2. What defines 'the amount'?

3. How does this created money 'get into circulation'?

Now we know the answer to (3) above is not that it is dropped from an airplane. Nor is it just because a bank may up and demand it (otherwise banks and building societies would not go out of business ... and what gives them a priority right to make such a demand, anyway?). (Although, of course, the recent bailouts were, precisely, 'because the banks demanded it'. But this is very unusual, as I'm sure you will agree. Hence all the furor)

If you want me to suggest answers for your consideration, answers that get to the heart of the matter, and may therefore explain to you what I consider to be the heart of the matter, then my considered understandings would be:

1. The precise mechanism for the creation of money is based on a Promissory Note, an IOU, signed by ANY individual when applying for a loan, mortgage, or equivalent. A 'promise to pay back'. (But, as you have already said, 'money is fiat, it has no value' ... so the 'pay back' is an empty promise ... just like the empty promise on a banknote itself)

2. The amount is the amount of the loan.

3. It is moved into circulation by making the amount available to whoever made the promise as a credit to an account on which s/he can draw upon. (Obviously, as you have explained, there are Statutory limits placed on this mechanism, such that it doesn't run off into infinity. For example by raising Interest Rates such that the Promissory Notes generated by loan applications (1) become fewer)

Now that is what I consider to be the heart of the matter. That's what I asked. Those are my understood answers.

Am I right or am I wrong?

Have I made my standpoint clear?

Kind regards + thanks for your kind attention,

Veronica: of the Chapman family

I received the response shown as Figure B7.

I decided to partially give up (although not completely), and sent back on passing shot:

Dear Paul: of the Morran family,

Thank you for your e-mail.

I specifically gave you the answers to the questions I actually asked, in terms of confirmation or denial. I did not wish to do that, because I did not wish to be accused of putting words into your mouth, preferring instead to rely on your intellectual honesty. But, as our correspondence progressed, you left me no choice.

You did not deny my suggested answers. But, of course, you did not confirm them either. I leave you to consider whether or not intellectual honesty reined supreme.

Anyway, I will assume you have done your best in very trying circumstances (i.e. 'someone like me'), and so I will just say thank you for the information you did provide.

The link to the Bank of England you supplied, goes to a page that mainly comprises Sponsorship Adverts and information about Interest Rates. I know I mentioned Interest Rates in my previous e-mail, but that was only in the nature of an example.

I care not one jot about any Rates of Interest, and did not ask any questions about them. Simply because the mechanism for creating money does not create sufficient to cover any Interest at all.

This leaves the entire economy (in total) in perpetual, never-ending, 'can-never-be-paid-off' debt - as I'm sure you can understand.

Or, perhaps you can tell me how the monies to create the Interest are produced? Well, no, because you refuse to confirm how the Principal is even created ... so I won't even bother to ask.

You hoped to 'allay my fears'. Did I give the impression I was fearful in any way? If so, then I humbly apologise. That was never my intent. I care not one jot about counterfeiting either. With respect, I think that is the Bank of England's problem, not mine. Any perceived value that results from counterfeiting activities is only the same as the perceived value of the banknotes themselves. And you have already told me the banknotes themselves are intrinsically worthless. Consequently those notes issued by the Bank of England have as much worth as counterfeit banknotes, do they not? So why is counterfeiting a problem?

No need to answer that last question because the only difference is that counterfeit notes are not issued under 'authority'. But whose authority ... that's the question. Which specific person provides, or specific persons provide, the authority? Do they work for HM Treasury? What are their names & Official Titles? And how do they decide how much fiat paper to authorise at any one time? And why? On what

basis is authority for issuance granted? That's what I asked - over an over again.

But it's quite plain those questions must remain officially unanswered.

Except that we know. That's how we knew what questions to ask, of course. Not confirmed ... but NOT denied.

I doubt you have heard the last of this because, as you so rightly say, others are catching on. For some reason they (a) Understand what I'm getting at and (b) Seem to think my questions are reasonable, and should be fully answered in detail.

Regards + thanks for your help, anyway,

Veronica: of the Chapman family.

What is the result of all this? Well, we have a flat denial that a **'Live Birth Trust Account'** exists. But we have no denial that it is not called by some other name: **'Exemption Account'**, or **'Redemption Account'** are two suggestions. We have a flat denial that this is tied to National Insurance Numbers, but we have no denial that it may be linked to Birth Certificate Numbers.

We have no denials because we have not asked these questions, in the appropriate way, is my best guess.

We have been given reasonable suspicion that the questions need to be asked in a specific way, otherwise denial is obviously possible. If you use the wrong name, then the fact that it does not exist is perfectly deniable.

We have no explanation for the fact that our National Insurance Numbers are required on just about every scrap of Officious Paperwork. We are left to wonder why that should be.

And we have not had a denial that my suggested answers to: *"How money is created"* were in any way incorrect. And denial would have been a piece of cake. All it would have amounted to was: *"I can confirm that you are wrong"*.

So, there it sits. At the time of writing. But, as Freemanship opens out, the answers will, I firmly believe, have to be forthcoming. The questions I have asked strike right into the heart of the illusion. One must expect a certain amount of resistance.

Figure B7: Fourth response from HM Treasury

HM TREASURY

1 Horse Guards Road London SW1A 2HQ

Information Rights Unit

Tel: 0207 270 4558
Fax: 0207 270 4861

www.hm-treasury.gov.uk
foi.responses@hm-treasury.gsi.gov.uk

Veronica: of the Chapman family

By email

Ref: 9/329

23 April 2009

Dear Veronica

Freedom of Information Act 2000: Money

Thank you for your enquiry dated 7 April. I am treating your request under the Freedom of Information Act 2000.

Following from your previous enquiries, you asked for information covering –

1. *what, precise, mechanism causes the release of 'some amount'? It must require some authority. Whose authority?*
2. *what defines 'the amount'?*
3. *how does this created money "get into circulation"?*

To the extent that the first two questions are addressed by recorded information we hold, I believe we have already pointed you to that information – the Currency Act 1983 requires Treasury authority, and sometimes notification to Parliament. The amount is defined in relation to amounts already in circulation and the unit is the pound sterling or approved subdivisions thereof.

In relation to the third part of your request, the Bank of England provides some detail on their arrangements at the following link, and they would be best placed to answer any more detailed points you might wish to raise.

http://www.bankofengland.co.uk/banknotes/about/distribution_circulation.htm

The commentary in your request focuses on the fact that currency has no inherent value. This is a theme that has been picked up by a number of other recent requests and some of these may be the people you know of who have been following our exchanges. In response, I have pointed out that although modern currency is tokenised, that doesn't stop forgers seeking to counterfeit such tokens, which is an indication of their perceived value. The system is regulated to prevent such abuse and ensure that the currency has confidence, so as to be exchangeable for valuable goods and services; it is these that ultimately value the currency.

I hope that view of things helps to allay your concerns.

Paul Morran
Information Rights Unit

But then, none of this should be a surprise. It appears that a genuinely-concerned MP, by the name of Stokes, had a go at trying to find out something, along similar lines, back in the 1940s. He did not succeed either. All he received were smarmy, devious, dismissive, responses.

Here's some Hansard on and around this subject:

UNITED KINGDOM CORPORATION.

HC Deb 22 October 1940 vol 365 c942W 942W

§ Mr. Craven-Ellis: asked the President of the Board of Trade whether the formation by the Government of the United Kingdom Corporation is only a war-time measure; and will he give assurance that the corporation will be wound up immediately after hostilities cease, so that the export trade may flow through its normal peace-time channels?

§ Mr. Johnstone: The corporation was formed with a view to meeting difficulties in overseas trade which are due to conditions arising out of the war. It is impossible to foresee the conditions that will obtain when hostilities cease and, therefore, I cannot say whether at that date it will be desirable to terminate the activities of the corporation. These activities do not, I think, disturb the normal channels of trade but I can assure my hon. Friend that His Majesty's Government have every desire that trade should be freed from war-time restrictions and be conducted in a normal manner at the earliest possible date.

UNITED KINGDOM COMMERCIAL CORPORATION

HC Deb 18 April 1944 vol 399 cc39-42W 40W

§ Mr. Parker :asked the Chancellor of the Exchequer if he will give a list of the names of the present directors of the United Kingdom Commercial Corporation, together with a list of other directorships which they hold.

§ Sir J. Anderson: The list of directors of the United Kingdom Commercial Corporation and of other directorships held by them is as follows:

[Please note: Many, if not all, of these people are now dead. The interesting part, for research purposes, is the Companies involved]

Sir Francis Joseph, Bt., K.B.E., D.L. (Acting Chairman) Directorships held:

Settle Speakman and Company Limited.
Mossfield Colliery Limited.
Bignall Hill Colliery Company Limited.
Stirrup and Pye Limited.
Fenton Collieries Limited.
Stafford Coal and Iron Company Limited.
Timber and Wood (Merseyside) Limited.
A. & S. Henry and Company Limited.
Blaw-Knox Limited.
London Midland and Scottish Railway Company Limited.
Birmingham Railway Carriage and Wagon Company Limited.
Midland Bank Limited.
Midland Bank Executor and Trustee Company Limited.
Rio Tinto Company Limited.
Birmingham Small Arms Company Limited.
Birmingham Canal Navigations.
Dundalk, Newry and Greenore Railway Company.

Mr. A. Chester Beatty Directorships held:

American Metal Company Limited.
Boart Products, Limited.
Consolidated African Selection Trust Limited.
Consolidated Diamond Mines of South West Africa Limited.
Mufulira Copper Mines Limited.
Northern Rhodesia Power Corporation Limited.
Rhodesian Selection Trust Limited.
Roan Antelope Copper Mines Limited.
Selection Trust Limited.
Seltrust Investments Limited.
Sierra Leone Selection Trust Limited.
Trepea Mines Limited.
Union Corporation Limited.
United Kingdom Commercial Corporation (Portugal) Limited.
Selection Manufacturing Company Limited.
Central Mining and Investment Corporation Limited.
Karamiat Estates Limited.

Freedom of Information interactions with HM Treasury

Mr. G. A. McEwen Directorships held:

Co-operative Wholesale Society Limited.
Chinese Purchasing Agency.
United Kingdom Commercial Corporation (Spain) Limited.
*Lord Swinton, Minister Resident in West Africa, still retains the post of Chairman of the Corporation.

Sir Frank Nixon Directorships held:

United Kingdom Commercial Corporation (Spain) Limited.
United Kingdom Commercial Corporation (Portugal) Limited.
United Kingdom Commercial Corporation (Ethiopia) Limited.
United Kingdom Commercial Corporation (Egypt) Limited.
United Kingdom Commercial Corporation (Eritrea) Limited.
United Kingdom Commercial Corporation (Iran) Limited.
United Kingdom Commercial Corporation (Iraq) Limited.
United Kingdom Commercial Corporation (Palestine) Limited.
United Kingdom Commercial Corporation (Sudan) Limited.
United Kingdom Commercial Corporation (Syria and Lebanon) Ltd.
United Kingdom Commercial Corporation (East Africa) Limited.

Mr. J. H. Hambro Directorships held:

Hambros Bank, Limited.
Hambro Trust, Limited.
Ashdown Investment Trust, Limited.
British and Continental Banking Company, Limited.
John Dickinson and Company, Limited.
United Kingdom Commercial Corporation (Spain), Limited.
United Kingdom Commercial Corporation (Portugal), Limited.
United Kingdom Commercial Corporation (Ethiopia), Limited.
United Kingdom Commercial Corporation (East Africa), Limited.
United Kingdom Commercial Corporation (Egypt), Limited.
United Kingdom Commercial Corporation (Eritrea), Limited.
United Kingdom Commercial Corporation (Iran), Limited.
United Kingdom Commercial Corporation (Iraq), Limited.
United Kingdom Commercial Corporation (Palestine), Limited.
United Kingdom Commercial Corporation (Sudan), Limited.
United Kingdom Commercial Corporation (Syria and Lebanon), Limited.

Mr. C. P. Lister Directorships held:

R. A. Lister and Company, Limited.
Blackstone and Company, Limited.
S.A. R. A. Lister et Cie.

Mr. L. C. Paton Directorships held:

Harrisons and Crosfield (Canada), Limited.
Harrisons and Crosfield (Borneo), Limited.
Harrisons, Barker and Company, Limited.
Wilkinson Rubber Linatex, Limited.
Wilkinson Sales Corporation (Canada), Limited.
British Borneo Timber Company, Limited.
United Kingdom Commercial Corporation (Portugal), Limited.
United Kingdom Commercial Corporation (Spain), Limited.

Captain J. A. Leighton Directorships held:

Stelp and Leighton, Limited.
J. H. Wackerbarth and Company, Limited. Southampton Steamship Company.
Crete Shipping Company.
Sark Motorships, Limited.
Guernsey, Alderney and Sark Steamship Company.
R. C. Hardman Sons, Limited.
United Kingdom Commercial Corporation (Portugal), Limited.
Lionel Edwards, Limited, Calcutta, India and any associated or subsidiary companies registered in India, Burma or Ceylon, and including the name "Lionel Edwards" in their title.
United Kingdom Commercial Corporation (Spain), Limited.

Mr. E. J. Shearer Directorships held:

Molyneux et Cie, Limited.
Survey and General Loan Company, Limited.

Mr. A. D. Campbell Directorships held:

Forbes, Campbell and Company, Limited.
George and R. Dewhurst, Limited.
Manchester Ship Canal Company.
Waring and Gillow (19312), Limited.
Martins Bank (Manchester Branch).

Manchester Chamber of Commerce.

Mr. E. H. Lever Directorships held:

Richard Thomas and Company, Limited.
Glasbrook Brothers, Limited.
Clayton Tin Plate Company, Limited.
Gravesend Steel and Tinplate Company, Limited.
H. F. Spencer and Company, Limited.
Lancaster's Steam Coal Collieries, Limited.
Monks, Hall and Company, Limited.
New Sharlston Collieries Company, Limited.
R.T. Metal Productions, Limited.
Richard Nevill and Company, Limited.
S. J. Burrell Prior, Limited.
South Wales Tinplate Corporation, Limited.
Swansea Navigation Collieries, Limited.
W. Gilbertson and Company, Limited.
Whitehead Thomas Bar and Strip Company, Limited.

New Money (Creation)

HC Deb 18 April 1944 vol 399 cc30-1 30

§ 58. Mr. Stokes: asked the Chancellor of the Exchequer whether he will in future have recourse to the creation of new money without interest instead of adding to the volume of bank advances to the Treasury as this would be no more inflationary and would cost the country less.

§ Sir J. Anderson: No, Sir.

§ Mr. Stokes: Will the Chancellor explain why it is preferable in the national interest to create new money with interest rather than create new money without?

§ Sir J. Anderson: My hon. Friend knows very well that I do not accept his monetary theories. He really cannot expect me to argue the matter with him at Question time.

New Money

HC Deb 27 April 1944 vol 399 cc924-5 924

§ Mr. Stokes: asked the Chancellor of the Exchequer how he keeps check of the amount of new money created.

§ The Chancellor of the Exchequer (Sir John Anderson): I do not find it necessary to attempt any such record as my hon. Friend suggests.

§ Mr. Stokes: But that is not an answer to my Question. Am I to understand from the Chancellor that he keeps no check on the amount of new money brought into circulation?

§ Sir J. Anderson: I keep no such check as my hon. Friend seems to have in mind. If he will study the White Paper, published on Tuesday—which he will find a veritable mine of information—perhaps he will then be good enough to indicate to me just what practical purpose he thinks such a record or check as he has in mind would serve.

§ Mr. Stokes: But is the Chancellor aware that competent authorities are of the opinion that something in the order of £1,500,000,000 has been created by the banks since the war began, at little cost to the banks and at great cost to the community? Does he not think it is his responsibility to see how much new money has been created? Surely it b a matter of business.

§ Sir J. Anderson: My hon. Friend referred to "competent authorities," but I am aware that the question of who is a competent authority is also a matter of opinion.

Government Stock (Interest Payments)

HC Deb 11 May 1944 vol 399 cc2086-7 2087

§ Mr. Graham White: asked the Financial Secretary to the Treasury if consideration has been given to the desirability of saving labour and paper by making arrangements for the payment of interest on 2½ per cent. Consols and other Trustee Securities by half-yearly instead of quarterly payments.

§ Mr. Assheton: Yes, Sir. As regards Government stocks on which dividends are paid quarterly, it has been established that in view of the limited amount of debt involved, no appreciable saving of labour or paper would be achieved by the suggested alteration. The arrangement has definite advantages, for certain classes of investors. A change of practice would require amendment of the law, and I do not think that a case has been made for it.

International Monetary Fund (Joint Statement)

HC Deb 16 May 1944 vol 400 c31 31

§ Mr. Stokes: asked the Chancellor of the Exchequer whether the British experts who collaborated in drawing up the Joint Statement by experts on the establishment of an International Monetary Fund were Treasury officials; and, if not, from what organisations were they selected.

§ Sir J. Anderson: Yes, Sir. Apart from Lord Keynes, the United Kingdom experts who collaborated in drawing up the Joint Statement were permanent Treasury officials and whole-time temporary officials who have been in the service of the Government throughout the war.

§ Mr. Stokes: Can the Chancellor assure the House that the whole-time temporary servants who have been in the employment of the Treasury for the period of the war are not drawn either from commercial or banking interests?

§ Sir J. Anderson: No, Sir, I do not think I could give such an assurance as that.

Appendix C: Magna Carta 1215

This is the Magna Carta 1215. The original one. It contains within it wording to the effect that it cannot be superseded. It stands behind all other Law, specifically Statute Law. The reason is simply that there was no such thing as 'Parliament' when this Treaty was enacted between the Nobility (at the time) and the Monarch (at the time – King John).

As a consequence any Parliamentary Statute is bound by it. Any Statute that attempts to supersede it is null & void in Law. This renders all Parliamentary Statutes either (a) Null & void or (b) Ineffective - since they can only quote Common Law anyway, and it is pointless to enforce something that is already in force as Law.

And this renders each and every one of the 111,000-plus Statutes, enacted on the basis of implementing EU Directives, as totally pointless wastes of time & effort.

All you have to do is **know. And stand up for yourself. You have an 'EU Referendum'. 24 hours per day, 7 days per week.**

Some of the most important sections of the Great Charter have been highlighted in ***bold italics:***

> John, by the grace of God, king of England, lord of Ireland, duke of Normandy and Aquitaine, and count of Anjou, to the archbishops, bishops, abbots, earls, barons, justiciars, foresters, sheriffs, stewards, servants, and to all his bailiffs and faithful subjects, greeting. Know that we, out of reverence for God and for the salvation of our soul and those of all our ancestors and heirs, for the honour of God and the exaltation of holy church, and for the reform of our realm, on the advice of our venerable fathers, Stephen, archbishop of Canterbury, primate of all England and cardinal of the holy Roman church, Henry archbishop of Dublin, William of London, Peter of Winchester, Jocelyn of Bath and Glastonbury, Hugh of Lincoln, Walter of Worcester, William of Coventry and Benedict of Rochester, bishops, of master Pandulf, subdeacon and member of the household of the lord pope, of brother Aymeric, master of the order of Knights Templar in England, and of the noble men William Marshal earl of Pembroke, William earl of Salisbury, William earl of Warenne, William earl of Arundel,

Alan of Galloway constable of Scotland, Warin fitz Gerold, Peter fitz Herbert, Hubert de Burgh seneschal of Poitou, Hugh de Neville, Matthew fitz Herbert, Thomas Basset, Alan Basset, Philip de Aubeney, Robert of Ropsley, John Marshal, John fitz Hugh, and others, our faithful subjects: [1] In the first place have granted to God, and by this our present charter confirmed for us and our heirs for ever that the English church shall be free, and shall have its rights undiminished and its liberties unimpaired; and it is our will that it be thus observed; which is evident from the fact that, before the quarrel between us and our barons began, we willingly and spontaneously granted and by our charter confirmed the freedom of elections which is reckoned most important and very essential to the English church, and obtained confirmation of it from the lord pope Innocent III; the which we will observe and we wish our heirs to observe it in good faith for ever.

We have also granted to all free men of our kingdom, for ourselves and our heirs for ever, all the liberties written below, to be had and held by them and their heirs, of us and our heirs for ever:

[2] If any of our earls or barons or others holding of us in chief by knight service dies, and at his death his heir be of full age and owe relief he shall have his inheritance on payment of the old relief, namely the heir or heirs of an earl £ 100 for a whole earl's barony, the heir or heirs of a baron £100 for a whole barony, the heir or heirs of a knight 100s, at most, for a whole knight's fee; and he who owes less shall give less according to the ancient usage of fiefs.

[3] If, however, the heir of any such be under age and a ward, he shall have his inheritance when he comes of age without paying relief and without making fine.

[4] The guardian of the land of such an heir who is under age shall take from the land of the heir no more than reasonable revenues, reasonable customary dues and reasonable services and that without destruction and waste of men or goods; and if we commit the wardship of the land of any such to a sheriff, or to any other who is answerable to us for its revenues, and he destroys or wastes what he has wardship of, we will take compensation from him and the land shall be committed to two lawful and discreet men of that fief, who shall be answerable for the revenues to us or to him to whom we have assigned them; and if we give or sell to anyone the wardship of any such land and he causes destruction or waste therein, he shall lose that wardship, and it shall be transferred to two lawful and discreet men of that fief, who shall similarly be answerable to us as is aforesaid.

[5] Moreover, so long as he has the wardship of the land, the guardian shall keep in repair the houses, parks, preserves, ponds, mills and other things pertaining to the land out of the revenues from it; and he shall restore to the heir when he comes of age his land fully stocked with ploughs and the means of husbandry according to what the season of husbandry requires and the revenues of the land can reasonably bear.

[6] Heirs shall be married without disparagement, yet so that before the marriage is contracted those nearest in blood to the heir shall have notice.

[7] A widow shall have her marriage portion and inheritance forthwith and without difficulty after the death of her husband; nor shall she pay anything to have her dower or her marriage portion or the inheritance which she and her husband held on the day of her husband's death; and she may remain in her husband's house for forty days after his death, within which time her dower shall be assigned to her.

[8] No widow shall be forced to marry so long as she wishes to live without a husband, provided that she gives security not to marry without our consent if she holds of us, or without the consent of her lord of whom she holds, if she holds of another.

[9] Neither we nor our bailiffs will seize for any debt any land or rent, so long as the chattels of the debtor are sufficient to repay the debt; nor will those who have gone surety for the debtor be distrained so long as the principal debtor is himself able to pay the debt; and if the principal debtor fails to pay the debt, having nothing wherewith to pay it, then shall the sureties answer for the debt; and they shall, if they wish, have the lands and rents of the debtor until they are reimbursed for the debt which they have paid for him, unless the principal debtor can show that he has discharged his obligation in the matter to the said sureties.

[10] If anyone who has borrowed from the Jews any sum, great or small, dies before it is repaid, the debt shall not bear interest as long as the heir is under age, of whomsoever he holds; and if the debt falls into our hands, we will not take anything except the principal mentioned in the bond.

[11] And if anyone dies indebted to the Jews, his wife shall have her dower and pay nothing of that debt; and if the dead man leaves children who are under age, they shall be provided with necessaries befitting the holding of the deceased; and the debt shall be paid out of the residue, reserving, however, service due to lords of the land; debts owing to others than Jews shall be dealt with in like manner.

[12] No scutage or aid shall be imposed in our kingdom unless by common counsel of our kingdom, except for ransoming our person, for making our eldest son a knight, and for once marrying our eldest daughter, and for these only a reasonable aid shall be levied. Be it done in like manner concerning aids from the city of London.

[13] And the city of London shall have all its ancient liberties and free customs as well by land as by water. Furthermore, we will and grant that all other cities, boroughs, towns, and ports shall have all their liberties and free customs.

[14] And to obtain the common counsel of the kingdom about the assessing of an aid (except in the three cases aforesaid) or of a scutage, we will cause to be summoned the archbishops, bishops, abbots, earls and greater barons, individually by our letters--and, in addition, we will cause to be summoned generally through our sheriffs and bailiffs all those holding of us in chief--for a fixed date, namely, after the expiry of at least forty days, and to a fixed place; and in all letters of such summons we will specify the reason for the summons. And when the summons has thus been made, the business shall proceed on the day appointed, according to the counsel of those present, though not all have come who were summoned.

[15] We will not in future grant any one the right to take an aid from his free men, except for ransoming his person, for making his eldest son a knight and for once marrying his eldest daughter, and for these only a reasonable aid shall be levied.

[16] No one shall be compelled to do greater service for a knight's fee or for any other free holding than is due from it.

[17] Common pleas shall not follow our court, but shall be held in some fixed place.

[18] Recognitions of novel disseisin, of mort d'ancester, and of darrein presentment, shall not be held elsewhere than in the counties to which they relate, and in this manner--we, or, if we should be out of the realm, our chief justiciar, will send two justices through each county four times a year, who, with four knights of each county chosen by the county, shall hold the said assizes in the county and on the day and in the place of meeting of the county court.

[19] And if the said assizes cannot all be held on the day of the county court, there shall stay behind as many of the knights and freeholders who were present at the county court on that day as are necessary for the sufficient making of judgments, according to the amount of business to be done.

[20] A free man shall not be amerced for a trivial offence except in accordance with the degree of the offence, and for a grave offence he shall be amerced in accordance with its gravity, yet saving his way of living; and a merchant in the same way, saving his stock-in-trade; and a villein shall be amerced in the same way, saving his means of livelihood--if they have fallen into our mercy: and none of the aforesaid amercements shall be imposed except by the oath of good men of the neighbourhood.

[21] Earls and barons shall not be amerced except by their peers, and only in accordance with the degree of the offence.

[22] No clerk shall be amerced in respect of his lay holding except after the manner of the others aforesaid and not according to the amount of his ecclesiastical benefice.

[23] No vill or individual shall be compelled to make bridges at river banks, except those who from of old are legally bound to do so.

[24] No sheriff, constable, coroners, or others of our bailiffs, shall hold pleas of our crown.

[25] All counties, hundreds, wapentakes and trithings shall be at the old rents without any additional payment, exept our demesne manors.

[26] If anyone holding a lay fief of us dies and our sheriff or bailiff shows our letters patent of summons for a debt that the deceased owed us, it shall be lawful for our sheriff or bailiff to attach and make a list of chattels of the deceased found upon the lay fief to the value of that debt under the supervision of law-worthy men, provided that none of the chattels shall be removed until the debt which is manifest has been paid to us in full; and the residue shall be left to the executors for carrying out the will of the deceased. And if nothing is owing to us from him, all the chattels shall accrue to the deceased, saving to his wife and children their reasonable shares.

[27] If any free man dies without leaving a will, his chattels shall be distributed by his nearest kinsfolk and friends under the supervision of the church, saving to every one the debts which the deceased owed him.

[28] No constable or other bailiff of ours shall take anyone's corn or other chattels unless he pays on the spot in cash for them or can delay payment by arrangement with the seller.

[29] No constable shall compel any knight to give money instead of castle-guard if he is willing to do the guard himself or through another good man, if for some good reason he cannot do it himself; and if we lead or send him on military service, he shall be excused guard in proportion to the time that because of us he has been on service.

[30] No sheriff, or bailiff of ours, or anyone else shall take the horses or carts of any free man for transport work save with the agreement of that freeman.

[31] Neither we nor our bailiffs will take, for castles or other works of ours, timber which is not ours, except with the agreement of him whose timber it is.

[32] We will not hold for more than a year and a day the lands of those convicted of felony, and then the lands shall be handed over to the lords of the fiefs.

[33] Henceforth all fish-weirs shall be cleared completely from the Thames and the Medway and throughout all England, except along the sea coast.

[34] The writ called Praecipe shall not in future be issued to anyone in respect of any holding whereby a free man may lose his court.

[35] Let there be one measure for wine throughout our kingdom, and one measure for ale, and one measure for corn, namely "the London quarter"; and one width for cloths whether dyed, russet or halberget, namely two ells within the selvedges. Let it be the same with weights as with measures.

[36] Nothing shall be given or taken in future for the writ of inquisition of life or limbs: instead it shall be granted free of charge and not refused.

[37] If anyone holds of us by fee-farm, by socage, or by burgage, and holds land of another by knight service, we will not, by reason of that fee-farm, socage, or burgage, have the wardship of his heir or of land of his that is of the fief of the other; nor will we have custody of the fee-farm, socage, or burgage, unless such fee-farm owes knight service. We will not have custody of anyone's heir or land which he holds of another by knight service by reason of any petty serjeanty which he holds of us by the service of rendering to us knives or arrows or the like.

[38] In future no official shall place a man on trial upon his own un-supported statement, without producing credible witnesses to the truth of it.

[39] No free man shall be seized or imprisoned, or stripped of his rights and possessions, or outlawed or exiled, or deprived of his standing in any other way, nor will we proceed with force against him, or send others to do so, except by the lawful judgement of his equals or by the law of the land.

[40] To no one will we sell, to no one deny or delay right or justice.

[41] All merchants shall be able to go out of and come into England safely and securely and stay and travel throughout England, as well by land as by water, for buying and selling by the ancient and right customs free from all evil tolls, except in time of war and if they are of the land that is at war with us. And if such are found in our land at the beginning of a war, they shall be attached, without injury to their persons or goods, until we, or our chief justiciar, know how merchants of our land are treated who were found in the land at war with us when war broke out, and if ours are safe there, the others shall be safe in our land.

[42] It shall be lawful in future for anyone, without prejudicing the allegiance due to us, to leave our kingdom and return safely and securely by land and water, save, in the public interest, for a short period in time of war--except for those imprisoned or outlawed in accordance with the law of the kingdom and natives of a land that is at war with us and merchants (who shall be treated as aforesaid).

[43] If anyone who holds of some escheat such as the honour of Wallingford, Nottingham, Boulogne, Lancaster, or of other escheats which are in our hands and are baronies dies, his heir shall give no other relief and do no other service to us than he would have done to the baron if that barony had been in the baron's hands; and we will hold it in the same manner in which the baron held it.

[44] Men who live outside the forest need not henceforth come before our justices of the forest upon a general summons, unless they are impleaded or are sureties for any person or persons who are attached for forest offences.

[45] We will appoint as justices, constables, sheriffs, or other officials, only men that know the law of the realm and are minded to keep it well

[46] All barons who have founded abbeys for which they have charters of the kings of England or ancient tenure shall have the custody of them during vacancies, as they ought to have.

[47] All forests that have been made forest in our time shall be immediately disafforested; and so be it done with riverbanks that have been made preserves by us in our time.

[48] All evil customs connected with forests and warrens, foresters and warreners, sheriffs and their officials, riverbanks and their wardens shall immediately be inquired into in each county by twelve sworn knights of the same county who are to be chosen by good men of the same county, and within forty days of the completion of the inquiry shall be utterly abolished by them so as never to be restored, provided that we, or our justiciar if we are not in England, know of it first.

[49] We will immediately return all hostages and charters given to us by Englishmen, as security for peace or faithful service.

[50] We will remove completely from office the relations of Gerard de Athée so that in future they shall have no office in England, namely Engelard de Cigogné, Peter and Guy and Andrew de Chanceaux, Guy de Cigogné, Geoffrey de Martigny and his brothers, Philip Marc and his brothers and his nephew Geoffrey, and all their following.

[51] As soon as peace is restored, we will remove from the kingdom all foreign knights, cross-bowmen, serjeants, and mercenaries, who have come with horses and arms to the detriment of the kingdom.

[52] If anyone has been disseised of or kept out of his lands, castles, franchises or his right by us without the legal judgment of his peers, we will immediately restore them to him: and if a dispute arises over this, then let it be decided by the judgment of the twenty-five barons who are mentioned below in the clause for securing the peace: for all the things, however, which anyone has been disseised or kept out of without the lawful judgment of his peers by king Henry, our father, or by king Richard, our brother, which we have in our hand or are held by others, to whom we are bound to warrant them, we will have the usual period of respite of crusaders, excepting those things about which a plea was started or an inquest made by our command before we took the cross; when however we return from our pilgrimage, or if by any chance we do not go on it, we will at once do full justice therein.

[53] We will have the same respite, and in the same manner, in the doing of justice in the matter of the disafforesting or retaining of the forests which Henry our father or Richard our brother afforested, and in the matter of the wardship of lands which are of the fief of another, wardships of which sort we have hitherto had by reason of a fief which anyone held of us by knight service, and in the matter of abbeys founded on the fief of another, not on a fief of our own, in which the lord of the fief claims he has a right; and when we have returned, or if we do not set out on our pilgrimage, we will at once do full justice to those who complain of these things.

[54] No one shall be arrested or imprisoned upon the appeal of a woman for the death of anyone except her husband.

[55]_All fines made with us unjustly and against the law of the land, and all amercements imposed unjustly and against the law of the land, shall be entirely remitted, or else let them be settled by the judgment of the twenty-five barons who are mentioned below in the clause for securing the peace [See Article 61], or by the judgment of the majority of the same, along with the aforesaid Stephen, archbishop of Canterbury, if he can be present, and such others as he may wish to associate with himself for this purpose, and if he cannot be present the business shall nevertheless proceed without him, provided that if any one or more of the aforesaid twenty-five barons are in a like suit, they shall be removed from the judgment of the case in question, and others chosen, sworn and put in their place by the rest of the same twenty-five for this case only.

[56] If we have disseised or kept out Welshmen from lands or liberties or other things without the legal judgment of their peers in England or in Wales, they shall be immediately restored to them; and if a dispute arises over this, then let it be decided in the March by the judgment of their peers--for holdings in England according to the law of England, for holdings in Wales according to the law of Wales, and for holdings in the March according to the law of the March. Welshmen shall do the same to us and ours.

[57] For all the things, however, which any Welshman was disseised of or kept out of without the lawful judgment of his peers by king Henry, our father, or king Richard, our brother, which we have in our hand or which are held by others, to whom we are bound to warrant them, we will have the usual period of respite of crusaders, excepting those things about which a plea was started or an inquest made by our command before we took the cross; when however we return, or if by any chance we do not set out on our pilgrimage, we will at once do full justice to them in accordance with the laws of the Welsh and the foresaid regions.

[58] We will give back at once the son of Llywelyn and all the hostages from Wales and the charters that were handed over to us as security for peace.

[59] We will act toward Alexander, king of the Scots, concerning the return of his sisters and hostages and concerning his franchises and his right in the same manner in which we act towards our other barons of England, unless it ought to be otherwise by the charters which we have from William his father, formerly king of the Scots, and this shall be determined by the judgment of his peers in our court.

[60] All these aforesaid customs and liberties which we have granted to be observed in our kingdom as far as it pertains to us towards our men, all of our kingdom, clerks as well as laymen, shall observe as far as it pertains to them towards their men.

[61] [Lawful Rebellion] Since, moreover, for God and the betterment of our kingdom and for the better allaying of the discord that has arisen between us and our barons we have granted all these things aforesaid, wishing them to enjoy the use of them unimpaired and unshaken for ever, we give and grant them the under-written security, namely, that the barons shall choose any twenty-five barons of the kingdom they wish, who must with all their might observe, hold and cause to be observed, the peace and liberties which we have granted and confirmed to them by this present charter of ours, so that if we, or our justiciar, or our bailiffs or any one of our servants offend in any way against anyone or transgress any of the articles of the peace or the security and the offence be notified to four of the aforesaid twenty-five barons, those four barons shall come to us, or to our justiciar if we are out of the kingdom, and, laying the transgression before us, shall petition us to have that transgression corrected without delay. ***And if we do not correct the transgression, or if we are out of the kingdom, if our justiciar does not correct it, within forty days, reckoning from the time it was brought to our notice or to that of our justiciar if we were out of the kingdom, the aforesaid four barons shall refer that case to the rest of the twenty-five barons and those twenty-five barons together with the community of the whole land shall distrain and distress us in every way they can, namely, by seizing castles, lands, possessions, and in***

such other ways as they can, saving our person and the persons of our queen and our children, until, in their opinion, amends have been made; and when amends have been made, they shall obey us as they did before. And let anyone in the land who wishes take an oath to obey the orders of the said twenty-five barons for the execution of all the aforesaid matters, and with them to distress us as much as he can, and we publicly and freely give anyone leave to take the oath who wishes to take it and we will never prohibit anyone from taking it. Indeed, all those in the land who are unwilling of themselves and of their own accord to take an oath to the twenty-five barons to help them to distrain and distress us, we will make them take the oath as aforesaid at our command. And if any of the twenty-five barons dies or leaves the country or is in any other way prevented from carrying out the things aforesaid, the rest of the aforesaid twenty-five barons shall choose as they think fit another one in his place, and he shall take the oath like the rest. In all matters the execution of which is committed to these twenty-five barons, if it should happen that these twenty-five are present yet disagree among themselves about anything, or if some of those summoned will not or cannot be present, that shall be held as fixed and established which the majority of those present ordained or commanded, exactly as if all the twenty-five had consented to it; and the said twenty-five shall swear that they will faithfully observe all the things aforesaid and will do all they can to get them observed. ***And we will procure nothing from anyone, either personally or through anyone else, whereby any of these concessions and liberties might be revoked or diminished; and if any such thing is procured, let it be void and null, and we will never use it either personally or through another.***

[62] And we have fully remitted and pardoned to everyone all the ill-will, indignation and rancour that have arisen between us and our men, clergy and laity, from the time of the quarrel. Furthermore, we have fully remitted to all, clergy and laity, and as far as pertains to us have completely forgiven, all trespasses occasioned by the same quarrel between Easter in the sixteenth year of our reign and the restoration of peace. And, besides, we have caused to be made for them letters testimonial patent of the lord Stephen archbishop of Canterbury, of the lord Henry archbishop of

Dublin and of the aforementioned bishops and of master Pandulf about this security and the aforementioned concessions.

[63] Wherefore we wish and firmly enjoin that the English church shall be free, ***and that the men in our kingdom shall have and hold all the aforesaid liberties, rights and concessions well and peacefully, freely and quietly, fully and completely, for themselves and their heirs from us and our heirs, in all matters and in all places for ever, as is aforesaid. An oath, moreover, has been taken, as well on our part as on the part of the barons, that all these things aforesaid shall be observed in good faith and without evil disposition. Witness the above-mentioned and many others. Given by our hand in the meadow which is called Runnymede between Windsor and Staines on the fifteenth day of June, in the seventeenth year of our reign.***

Appendix D: Notice of Understanding and Intent and Claim of Right

You can make your own Law. Law that applies only to you. It is (basically) an Affidavit and an Oath combined. A Statement of Truth ... as you see it. Provided it is not objected to, in the manner described in the Chapter on *Noticing*, then it becomes Your Truth.

Even though you may be wrong. Remember: If you were wrong then it should have received objections within the stated time period.

Quite obviously you cannot claim Rights that are otherwise unavailable to you under Common Law. You cannot, for example, claim the Right to breach the peace, murder someone, or defraud someone. However what you can do is to state specific instances of what you consider the Truth to be ... in your specific case.

You do this by stating what you understand the situation to be. You then state, categorically, your intention to live in peaceful co-existence with everyone else. You then make claims based on that.

You provide this Notice to whomsoever you think needs to know. You can use the maxim of: *"Service to Principal is considered service to Agent, and service to Agent is considered service to Principal"*. This means that, in any organisation, one hand is responsible for telling the other hand what is going on.

I now include (below) my own, which was sent to the UK Home Office in March, 2009. I did not get any response, and thus received no objections in the time period.

Of course, they were just ignoring me ... as if I didn't count. However the test will come should anything untoward happen to me.

Each clause is numbered. I did this in order to resolve any objections easily. I included a Fee Schedule for any transgressions against me. I used 'terms of imprisonment', but could have set 'monetary amounts'. The terms of imprisonment can be anything I choose, and any monetary amounts likewise. I did not set monetary amounts for the simple reason that 'money' is an illusion.

This was sent with an appropriate covering letter explaining the need to create any necessary 'services to Agents'. My NOUICOR (as it is called for short) is on the following pages. It should be noted that I do not have to exercise all the Claims I have made. They can be left in abeyance for as long as I determine the need to leave them unused. These are My Claims. My Rights. I can utilise them in whatever way I choose, and as I see fit.

Notice of Understanding and Intent and Claim of Right

I, Veronica: of the Chapman family, hereinafter known as Veronica: Chapman, a flesh and blood human being in possession of a sovereign and individual spirit, a living soul, do hereby make Oath and state the following is My Truth and My Law:

[010] Whereas it is my understanding that in terms of earthly existence there is no species more supreme than a living, breathing, imaginative human being blessed with a living soul, and

[020] Whereas it is my understanding that it is impossible to distinguish one soul from any other, and therefore all souls must at all times and in all situations be considered equal in all respects in any fair, just and reasonable context, and

[030] Whereas it is my understanding that anything and everything must in practice derive from the aforesaid axioms, and

[040] Whereas it is my understanding that any numerical grouping of such souls can be referred to as 'people', and

[050] Whereas it is my understanding that a society is, in essence, nothing more than a grouping of like-minded souls since it is defined as a number of people joined by mutual consent to deliberate, determine and act for a common goal, and

[060] Whereas it is my understanding a statute is defined as a legislated rule of a society, and

[070] Whereas it is my understanding a legislated rule of a society can be given the force of law to act upon, or lawfully bind, all members of that society, and

[080] Whereas it is my understanding if a living soul chooses by free will not to be a member of any society then statutes created by said society do not bind that soul to said statute law, and

[090] Whereas it is my understanding a living soul who chooses by free will not to be a member of any society can be referred to as a Freeman-on-the-land, and

[100] Whereas it is my understanding a Freeman-on-the-land remains entirely and solely under Common Law jurisdiction, and

[110] Whereas I Veronica: Chapman am a Freeman-on-the-land, and

Notice of Understanding and Intent and Claim of Right

[120] Whereas it is my understanding that all authority possessed by elected representatives must inherently derive from those who elect said representation, and

[130] Whereas it is my understanding that if I have the right to empower representation by casting a vote then I am empowered to represent myself, and

[140] Whereas it is my understanding that the right of empowerment does not derive from any government otherwise it would be possible for a government to revoke it, and

[150] Whereas it is my understanding that if the right to empower representation were revoked then no representation would thereafter be possible, and

[160] Whereas it is my understanding the only form of government recognized as lawful in the United Kingdom is a representative one, and,

[170] Whereas it is my understanding representation requires mutual consent, and

[180] Whereas it is my understanding that in the absence of mutual consent neither representation nor governance can exist, and

[190] Whereas it is my understanding the United Kingdom is a Common Law jurisdiction enjoying the protection of Common Law, and

[200] Whereas it is my understanding equality before the law is paramount and mandatory, and

[210] Whereas it is my understanding that for something to exist legally it must have a name, and

[220] Whereas it is my understanding that the UNITED KINGDOM is in reality a corporation in Chapter 11 bankruptcy and thus still allowed to trade, and

[230] Whereas it is my understanding that by virtue of my birth within the boundaries of my Country England I am a single share owner in said UNITED KINGDOM CORPORATION, and

[240] Whereas it is my understanding all Acts are statutes restricted in scope and applicability by the British Constitution and Common Law, and

[250] Whereas it is my understanding a statute being defined as a legislated rule of a society is, within the United Kingdom, in fact a rule of said UNITED KINGDOM CORPORATION, and

[260] Whereas it is my understanding rules of a corporation are limited in applicability to those who are agents of said corporation, and

[270] Whereas it is my understanding those who have a National Insurance Number are in fact employees of the government and thus are bound by the statutes created by the said government, and

[280] Whereas it is my understanding that it is lawful to abandon one's National Insurance Number while at the same time not affecting the right to any pension claim based on National Insurance Contributions previously paid, and

[290] Whereas it is my understanding people in the United Kingdom have a right to revoke or deny consent to be represented and thus governed, and

[300] Whereas it is my understanding if anyone does revoke or deny consent they exist free of government control and statutory restraints, and

[310] Whereas it is my understanding that a claim of right establishes a lawful excuse, and

[320] Whereas it is my understanding that if one has lawful excuse one may choose to not obey a court, tribunal, statute, Act or order, and

[330] Whereas a Freeman-on-the-Land has lawfully revoked consent and does exist free of statutory restrictions, obligations, and limitations, and

[340] Whereas it is my understanding that I, Veronica: Chapman as a Freeman-on-the-Land, acting peacefully within community standards, would not in that capacity breach the peace, and

[350] Whereas it is my understanding that all existing courts and governments are de facto only and not de jure, and

[360] Whereas it is my understanding that a woman acting as Elizabeth Alexandra Mary Windsor did take the throne of England on the Second Day of June, Nineteen Hundred and Fifty Three, and

[370] Whereas it is my understanding that during a Coronation ceremony said woman acting as Elizabeth Alexandra Mary Windsor was asked by a man acting in the role of the then Archbishop of Canterbury "Will you solemnly promise and swear to govern the Peoples of the United Kingdom of Great Britain and Northern Ireland, Canada, Australia, New Zealand, the Union of South

Africa, Pakistan, and Ceylon, and of your Possessions and the other Territories to any of them belonging or pertaining, according to their respective laws and customs?" and she responded "I solemnly promise so to do", and

[380] Whereas it is my understanding that this ceremony did install said woman as Queen of England and the United Kingdom, and

[390] Whereas it is my understanding that on or after the Seventeenth Day of October Nineteen Hundred and Seventy Two said woman did sign into statute an Act of Parliament known as the European Communities Act of Nineteen Hundred and Seventy Two (ECA1972) which accepted without my consent a treaty known as the Treaty of Rome, and

[400] Whereas it is my understanding that the terms of the Treaty of Rome are counter in many respects to the "respective laws and customs" of those nations of which said woman is Queen including England which is my Country of birth, and

[410] Whereas it is my understanding that anyone who participates in allowing or by culpable neglect enabling my Country to be governed in any way by any foreign power is an act of treason as defined by the British Constitution, and

[420] Whereas it is my understanding, therefore, that by signing of the ECA1972 as opposed to dissolving by Royal Prerogative the Parliament that created the treacherous Act was in itself by collusion an attempted act of treason against my Country, and

[430] Whereas it is my understanding that as a Freeman-on-the-Land in this common law jurisdiction that I have the duty to stand in defence of the United Kingdom and its people against foreign armed troops who attempt to invade, govern or police me or my Country, and

[440] Whereas it is my understanding that this duty is not affected by agreements made by treasonous and de facto government agents, and

[450] Whereas it is my understanding that agreements made on behalf of the United Kingdom by traitors to the United Kingdom do not bind the people of United Kingdom, and

[460] Whereas I do firmly and truly believe the aforementioned agreement is an overt act of treason, and

[470] Whereas I honourably refuse to be bound by agreements made by traitors such as said Elizabeth Alexandra Mary Windsor in collusion with the then Prime Minister Edward Heath, and

[480] Whereas it is my understanding that any peace officer who co-operates with foreign armed troops to govern or regulate the population is also committing treason, and

[490] Whereas it is my understanding that historically the purpose of a national armed force was to ensure that foreign powers never invaded and governed under a gun, and

[500] Whereas it is my understanding that the existence of armed foreign troops patrolling and policing our streets would be evidence of a war fought unsuccessfully, and

[510] Whereas it is my understanding that agreeing or conspiring to agree to allow armed foreign troops to patrol and police our streets is an act of treason, and

[520] Whereas it is my understanding that any action for which one can apply for and receive a licence must itself be a fundamentally lawful action, and

[530] Whereas as I not a child and I am a Freeman-on-the-Land who operates with full responsibility and I do not see the need to ask permission to engage in lawful and peaceful activities, especially from those who claim limited liability, and

[540] Whereas it is my understanding that I have a right to use my property without having to pay for the use or enjoyment of it, and

[550] Whereas it is my understanding that all 'public transportation' is in fact and actuality public property to which I have the right of use and access without having to pay, and

[560] Whereas it is my understanding peace officers have a duty to distinguish between statutes and law and those who attempt to enforce statutes against a Freeman-on-the-Land are in fact breaking the law, and

[570] Whereas it is my understanding that I have the power to refuse intercourse or interaction with peace officers who have not observed me breach the peace, and

[580] Whereas it is my understanding that permanent estoppel by acquiescence barring any peace officer or prosecutor from bringing charges against a Freeman-on-the-Land under any Act is created if this claim is not responded to in the stated fashion and time, and

Notice of Understanding and Intent and Claim of Right

[590] Whereas it is my understanding that the Common Law right to travel on the highways without license provided one is not engaging in commerce thereupon is lawful and still exists although it does appear to have been deceptively hidden, and

[600] Whereas the Road Traffic Acts of the United Kingdom do make it possible for peace officers in the role of policy enforcement officers to stop an automobile in order to provide services and demand something of value, and

[610] Whereas it is my understanding that if they are not providing a service they have no reason to stop any one and if proof of registration, insurance and licence is not valuable they have no need to ask for it, and

[620] Whereas it is my understanding that I have the right to refuse to interact or co-operate with criminals, de facto government agents or grossly negligent peace officers, and

[630] Whereas it is my understanding that if I have the power to elect a representative and empower them to appoint peace officers then I also have the power to appoint directly, and

[640] Whereas it is my understanding that if I have the power to appoint directly or by proxy I must have the power to fulfil those duties my self, and

[650] Whereas it is my understanding that the United Kingdom Police Force although having an illustrious history has had members recently acting in a grossly criminal manner which does tarnish the previous history and record, and

[660] Whereas it is my understanding that the Law provides remedy at all times, even against rogue or negligent peace officers and de facto governments apparently hijacked by soulless corporate interests, and

[670] Whereas it is my understanding that in order to be a peace maker and deal with rogue and possibly armed police officers who fail to act with respect to the code of Common Law I will need use of and access to firearms of equal or greater power then those people who act criminally have access to, and

[680] Whereas it is my understanding that the act of registering the birth of a baby creates a legal entity called a person that exists in association with that baby and that the manner in which offspring are registered transfers superior guardianship rights over that offspring to the government, and

[690] Whereas it is my understanding that this creation of a person and transfer of authority is not fully disclosed to the parents and if it was all good parents would refuse to register their offspring, and

[700] Whereas it is my understanding that the person and the human being to which it is associated are two very separate and different things and that the people playing roles in government only have the right to act upon the person, and

[710] Whereas it is my understanding that if I do not exist in association with a person I cannot be lawfully governed by the people playing roles in government, and

[720] Whereas it is my understanding a by-law is defined as a rule of a corporation, and

[730] Whereas it is my understanding corporations are legal fictions and require contracts in order to claim authority or control over other parties, and

[740] Whereas it is my understanding that a summons is merely an invitation to attend and those issued by the Ministry of Justice or its franchises which are de facto corporations create no obligation or dishonour if ignored, and

[750] Whereas it is my understanding legal fictions lack a soul and cannot exert any control over those who are thus blessed and operate with respect to that knowledge as only a fool would allow soulless fictions to dictate one's actions, and

[760] Whereas it is my understanding that the people in the government are merely playing roles, and

[770] Whereas I AM NOT PLAYING, and

[780] Whereas it is my understanding that I am not obliged to obey the orders of any one claiming to be a Queen or King or those acting on behalf of such an insane entity, as no one who does make preposterous claims that abandon and erode the concept of equality has any authority over me, and

[790] Whereas it is my understanding that I can use a Notary Public to perform duties found under any Act including thus they have the power to hold court and hear evidence and issue binding lawful judgments, and

[800] Whereas it is my understanding that a Notary Public can also be used to bring criminal charges to bear against traitors, even if they hold the highest office, and

Notice of Understanding and Intent and Claim of Right

[810] Whereas it is my understanding that there may be more of this to follow

[820] Therefore be it now known to any and all interested, concerned or affected parties, that I, Veronica: Chapman am a Freeman-on-the-Land and do hereby serve notice and state clearly specifically and unequivocally my intent to peacefully and lawfully exist free of all statutory obligations, restrictions and that I maintain all rights at law to trade, exchange or barter and exist without deceptive governance and to do so without limitations, restrictions or regulations created by others and without my consent.

[830] Be it also now known to any and all interested, concerned or affected parties, that I, Veronica: Chapman as a Freeman-on-the-Land and do hereby serve notice and state clearly specifically and unequivocally that I would never conspire nor would I in any way entreat others to disobey the Common Law of the Land which ensures peaceful co-existence.

[840] Furthermore, I claim that these actions are not outside my communities' standards and will in fact support said community in our desire for truth and maximum freedom.

[850] Furthermore, I claim the right to engage in these actions and further claim that all property held by me is held under a claim of right.

[860] Furthermore, I claim that anyone who interferes with my lawful activities after having been served notice of this claim and who fails to properly dispute or make lawful counterclaim is breaking the law, cannot claim good faith or colour of right and that such transgressions will be dealt with in a properly convened court de jure.

[870] Furthermore, I claim it is my right and solemn duty not only to keep the peace My Self but also to intervene wherever may be necessary to ensure that the peace is kept in a situation where peace officers are not present or are unwilling for whatever reason to uphold their sworn and solemn duty so to do.

[880] Furthermore, I claim that the identity of My Self is forever possible to establish correctly by my Presence as a living, breathing, Human Being with a soul together as may be necessary sworn attestations from friends, family, and other associates. Furthermore I claim that this supersedes any necessity to obtain or carry any form of external token such as an Identity Card for any lawful purpose of establishing my true identity for the simple reason that

no such token can ever represent the sovereign soul with which I am blessed.

[890] Furthermore, I claim that the courts in The United Kingdom are de-facto and bound by the Law and Equity Acts and are in fact in the profitable business of conducting, witnessing and facilitating the transactions of security interests and I further claim they require the consent of both parties prior to providing any such services.

[900] Furthermore, I claim all transactions of security interests require the consent of both parties and I do hereby deny consent to any transaction of a security interest issuing under any Act for as herein stated as a Freeman-on-the-Land I am not subject to any Act.

[910] Furthermore I claim ownership of my single share in the corporation known as the UNITED KINGDOM and demand a copy of said share such that I will become the shareholder and thereby be in the position of exercising my own voting rights. Furthermore I claim to receive the corresponding dividends for as long as said UNITED KINGDOM operates under the illusion that 'money has some value' (notwithstanding the fact that 'money has no value' has been admitted by HM Treasury. Evidence of this admission can be supplied, and is anyway publicly available).

[920] Furthermore I claim that my inalienable Natural Right to Trial By Jury for any apparent transgressions on my part, including an inalienable Natural Right of Habeas Corpus, and these shall not under any circumstances be infringed.

[930] Furthermore I claim the right to be entirely free to determine my own medication needs at all times and never under any circumstances be forced to ingest or otherwise receive into my body by way of vaccination, electro-magnetic energy, audio or visual energy or any other method any substance or alien energies I do not consent to accept.

[940] Furthermore, I claim the right to convene a proper court de jure in order to address any potentially criminal actions of any peace officers, government principals or agents or justice system participants who having been served notice of this claim fail to dispute or discuss or make lawful counterclaim and then interfere by act or omission with the lawful exercise of properly claimed and established rights and freedoms.

Notice of Understanding and Intent and Claim of Right

[950] Furthermore, I claim the right to fulfil my duty to shoot any foreign troops in the United Kingdom who are armed and attempting to police or govern me or my fellow countrymen without consent and to view them as an invading force which must be lawfully attacked. And I further claim to right to nominate as many deputies as may be necessary who by their own free will and consent are prepared to assist me in fulfilment of this duty to my Country.

[960] Furthermore, I claim the law of agent and principal applies and that service upon one is service upon both.

[970] Furthermore, I claim the right to deal with any counterclaims or disputes publicly and in an open forum using discussion and negotiation and to capture on video tape said discussion and negotiation for whatever lawful purpose as I see fit.

[980] Furthermore, I claim my SCHEDULE for any transgressions by peace officers, government principals or agents or justice system participants or agents of the medical profession or any other parties who trespass upon and thus unlawfully hinder My Peaceful Self, Veronica: of the Chapman family, as defined in attached Schedule A.

[990] Furthermore I claim the right to use a Notary Public to conduct due process of the aforementioned SCHEDULE against any transgressors who by their actions or omissions harm me or my interests, directly or by proxy in any way.

Affected parties wishing to dispute the claims made herein or make their own counterclaims must respond appropriately within FOURTEEN (14) days of service of notice of this action. Responses must be under Oath or Attestation, upon full commercial liability and penalty of perjury and registered at the Place of Claim of Right provided no later than fourteen days from the date of original service as attested to by way of certificate of service. Schedule B is available for the resolution of any objections.

Failure to register a dispute against the claims made herein and then successfully defeating these claims in a proper court of law will result in an automatic default judgment securing forevermore all rights herein claimed and establishing permanent and irrevocable estoppel by acquiescence barring the bringing of charges under any statute or Act or regulation against My Self Freeman-on-the-Land Veronica: Chapman for exercising these lawful and properly established rights, freedoms and duties.

Place of Claim of Right: ______________________________

Dated: ______________________________

Claimant: Veronica: of the Chapman family

____

____

Independent Witness 1: ______________________________

Address: ______________________________

____

____

____

____

Independent Witness 2: ______________________________

Address: ______________________________

____

____

____

____

Independent Witness 3: ______________________________

Address: ______________________________

____

____

____

Notice of Understanding and Intent and Claim of Right

Schedule A

Penalty term of imprisonment to apply to each and every individual reasonably involved in the transgression, including all senior officers or line managers as accomplices in law.

Transgression	Penalty Term of Imprisonment
My Self being questioned, interrogated or in any way detained, harassed or otherwise regulated	1 year
My Self handcuffed, transported, incarcerated or subjected to any adjudication process that is outside Common Law jurisdiction	2 years
My Self forced to suffer the effects of what has come to be known as a non-lethal or less-than-lethal weapon such as a Taser	5 years
My Self forced to undergo any ingestion of energies or substances forced onto or into my body, whether under to guise of medication or not, without my expressly notarised consent	10 years
My Self being attributed anything I did not actually speak or write in the event that my written or spoken communications are shown to be tampered with	5 years.

Schedule B

Objections and Resolutions.

Notice of Understanding and Intent and Claim of Right

Schedule C

Supportive Understandings.

Schedule D

Additional Claims.

Appendix E: Summary of Freeman Principles

There is a lot of information in this book, and it may take a few reads in order for the whole situation to sink in. You may also find the need to explain to others. I write this Appendix for those reasons, fundamentally to explain exactly 'where the Freeman is coming from'

It goes like this.

A Statute is "a legislated rule of a Society".

A Society is "a group of like-minded individuals who come together to deliberate, determine, and act towards common goals".

Those are the definitions. A dictionary can be consulted in order to verify them.

For anything to exist in Law it must have a Name, to which it can be referred.

As far as a Society is concerned, it must also have a Membership.

Individuals apply for Membership when they consider the "common goals" are those they can support.

For this to occur, the Society must have defined its goals in the first place ... such that Applicants can know whether or not the "common goals" are those that can be supported by Membership.

If, at any time, a Member determines that he or she can no longer support the Society's espoused goals, then he or she has the ability to RESIGN Membership.

That's a Society, and Statues are the legislated rules it sets for itself. Application for Membership is an application to agree to be bound by the Society's rules.

Since Statutes only bind CURRENT Members of any Society, ***they have no affect on non-Members***.

This is identical to the Policy (Company Rules) of any Company, since a Company is the same thing as a Society. ***Fundamentally, in terms of 'status'***, the employees of a Company are indistinguishable from Members of a Society.

So, before Statutes can be used to bind an individual in Law, a number of proofs need to be forthcoming:

1. Proof that the Society has a Legal Name, by which it can be uniquely identified;

2. Proof that the Society has set, and published, its Common Goals;

3. Proof that the individual has applied for Membership, and said application was accepted;

4. Proof that the individual has not subsequently resigned.

Subject to all of the above proofs, an individual is bound, in Law, by the Statutes of the Society of which s/he is a Member. In this case, by applying for Membership, the individual CONSENTED TO BE BOUND.

If any one of the above cannot be proved, then an individual is only bound, in Law, by the Statutes of the Society, IF HE OR SHE CONSENTS TO BE BOUND.

In any/all other cases, the individual is not bound by the Society's Statutes, in Law.

So ... before going any further ... indeed before taking one more breath ... the above statements need to be rebutted IN SUBSTANCE ... or, by silence and/or lack of rebuttal ... ACCEPTED. That's by anyone, and everyone, with whom we may be forced to interact.

'Legal obligations' are always addressed to a Named Party.

You are not a Name. You are a sovereign flesh & blood Human Being, with a living soul, and not a Legal Fiction Name, such as "MISS VERONICA CHAPMAN" (or any variation).

You are not a Name, because a Name is merely marks on paper, pixels on a computer screen, or sound pressure waves in the air, when spoken.

Now, some may ask: "What's the difference?" But the difference is enormous. It's the difference between the marks on the paper (etc.), and a flesh & blood creature that is 'aware' - in other words something that is 'conscious'.

Now, the point is - and this is what it is really all about (if you think about it): How do you grab the attention of a creature that is 'aware'? When you want that attention? How do you grab the attention of a flesh & blood creature?

Well ... simple ... you CALL IT! You CALL it by 'what it is commonly called'!

This one, the one writing this book, is COMMONLY CALLED as: *"Veronica"*! And, since there is more than one Veronica in the world, the

Summary of Freeman Principles

Caller may need to be a bit more specific … and so add my clan/tribe/family to the calling, and to call: *"Veronica: of the Chapman family"*.

When I'm CALLED this way, you get my attention! Hey! It works!

The Legal Fiction Names used, e.g. "MISS VERONICA CHAPMAN" (and so on), are actually the Names of little ships. Little ships that the Vatican considers it owns. When one writes to these little ships, they should send their letters to the Vatican, not to me.

Why does the Vatican do this (via the UK Government)? Very simply because most people think that they are their Legal Fiction Name, and respond accordingly. This places them, by tacit consent, as CONSENTING MEMBERS TO THE STATUTES QUOTED.

It's a deception, of course. One is never told this, is one? Well, they never told me, but we've found out. So the deceptions don't work any more. (The Internet is a wonderful thing, if used for something other than just typing "big tits" into a Search Engine)

Here's one more point. A Name is not the flesh & blood. A Name is ATTACHED to the flesh & blood. Usually by one's parents, at birth. You "GIVE the child a Name", don't you? You GIVE it a Name. It doesn't have one, as the flesh & blood comes into the world, so you GIVE it a Name.

The Name is ATTACHED. And this is provable by the fact that a Deed Poll can DETACH a Name, and ATTACH a different one. (Just the same as re-naming a ship, where the old name is blotted out, and the new one painted over).

If someone says to me: *"Are you Veronica Chapman?"* … the truthful answer is: *"No, I'm not a Name"*.

If someone says to me: *"Are you the flesh & blood sovereign Human Being, with a living soul, to which the Name Veronica Chapman is ATTACHED,* ***at this moment in time****?"* … then I have to say: *"Yes, it seems like that"*, in order to remain truthful.

(But I'm never asked that question, in that way. Am I?)

My Self, the Human Being, the flesh & blood, attention grabbed by calling Veronica: of the Chapman family, remains solely under the Common Law jurisdiction of England.

Provided I do not:

1. Breach the peace;
2. Cause deliberate harm to anyone else;

3. Cause deliberate loss to anyone else;
4. Use deviousness in my promises & agreements …

… then I do not violate any tenet of Common Law. And, if anyone thinks that I may have done, then the mechanism of Trial by Jury exists to try me, and find me innocent or guilty, as its verdict. Doesn't it?

They can take me to Court if they like. But I'll just claim Common Law jurisdiction, and ask the Court if it has Common Law jurisdiction. Unless there is a Jury sitting, the Court will have to answer: *"No"*. So I will ask the Court what jurisdiction it has over My Self. And it will be forced to admit that, while it may have jurisdiction over the MATTER, it has NONE over My Self whatsoever.

Obviously I would be asking the Court to prove that I am a CURRENT Member of the Society whose subsisting regulations the Claimant & the Court are attempting to impose … so they'd better be ready to rebut just about everything I wrote about Statutes & Societies, above. This might cause them a bit of a problem, since what I wrote was the plain, unvarnished, truth.

No Statute is above Common Law. Statutes are ***bound by*** Common Law. If they exceed Common Law, ***then they are null & void***. And that's the Law-of-the-LAND (which is Common Law … and actually nothing more than Common Sense).

The reason for this is simple. Common Law/Common Sense was around long before 'Parliament' and 'Government' were invented. These entities were invented ***under*** Common Law/Common Sense … ***not above it***.

'Not above it', because only a complete pillock would ever claim to somehow "Do better than Common Sense", surely? Consequently only such a pillock would claim that Parliament could "Do better than Common Sense/Common Law". So, what is Parliament doing? You tell me! It certainly isn't "Doing better than Common Sense", is it? Because that's impossible, isn't it?

Any argument to the effect that, because I have a vote, I am somehow bound by the Statutes, is entirely spurious. For the following reason. Before any Member of Parliament can take a seat in the House of Commons, they must swear allegiance to the reigning Monarch. Not to those poor suckers who did their so-called 'civil duty', and put an "X" against said MP's Name. Consequently the allegiance of those 650+ showers of shit is not to you & I, it is to the Queen. She might very well be bound by what they decide, but - since their allegiance is not to you & I - we are not so bound.

Summary of Freeman Principles

How can we be? If Human "A" makes a promise to Human "B", Human "C" is not bound by that promise.

I'll just throw in a couple of other maxims from old Roman Law (we were under Roman Occupation at one time in our history).

The first one is "Consensus Facit Legem" … which, translated, means "CONSENT MAKES LAW". Consent. Consent! The Law can only be made by consent. How many people, do you think, would consent to pay Income Tax, Road Tax/SORN etc. if anyone actually dared to ask directly? Bear in mind what I've written about the Grand Deception of 'money'.

Why, do you think, the Government is so shit-scared of any Referendum? On anything? The EU, Road Tax … anything?

Because they would not obtain consent. And the majority know that, as well as I do. The Irish most certainly do, as in: *"Keep voting Ireland … we will grind you down until you say "Yes""*. They can only gain consent by grinding us down. (However, the consent is really just a plea to "stop the grinding").

Consent makes Law … and they do not have consent. You know it. I know it.

The other maxim is "Let he who will be deceived, be deceived".

So don't be deceived.

And then we have 'Contracts'. We are constantly DECEIVED into making Contracts we did not realise we were making. However, any and all Contracts we have been DECEIVED into making are null & void, IN LAW, on the basis of:

1. Lack of full disclosure by the other Party

2. Lack of any Contractual Consideration being offered by the other Party entirely from its own resources.

3. Lack of lawful Terms & Conditions, under Common Law. The deceptions are crimes under Common Law.

And one final, final thing. If anyone thinks - for one second - that all a Freeman is doing is trying to 'tax-dodge', then they'd need to think that again, on top of everything else.

And here's the reason.

The so-called 'Government' was elected to look after the roads, infrastructure & health care etc. And to ***protect*** our freedoms … not to continuously deceive us by means of faux Belief Systems.

As such, they are given the power to create a 'Monetary illusion', via HM Treasury. We let them create whatever they decide they need. Don't we? (How/where does money come from then?)

So, if ANY Government Agency (e.g. HM Revenue & Customs) wants money, then they can get all they need from the MAKERS ... HM Treasury! They are the ones who make it! ***Don't ask us! Why ask us? We don't make it!***

Tell me ... why can't HM Revenue & Customs, and the DVLA, etc. get all their money from those who create it?

Why do they need to bother us?

What, precisely, is the point in bothering me? Or any of us? We elect the Government to look after these things ... we give them the power to create as much 'money' as they would ever need ... and the very first thing they do is demand it from us!!!

Huh???!!! If it wasn't so bloody serious, and utterly, preposterously, absurd, it would actually be hilarious!

It's perfectly true, isn't it? Plain Common Sense, isn't it?

(And the answer, by the way, is that 'the money' has to pass through us for one reason, and one reason only: TO CONTROL US. 'Money' is nothing more - and nothing less - than a ***Mind-Fuck***. It serves no other ***practical*** purpose).

The sooner everyone comes to terms with this, and stops deceiving people, the better for all concerned. As the deceptions become more & more exposed, I just hope the Great British Public (in fact everyone on this planet) has mercy on the souls of these so-called 'Government Agencies'.

Now it's been said. No-one, having read this, can claim ignorance any longer.

Unless and until these Freeman Principles are rebutted, IN SUBSTANCE, they stand as the REALITY, and the TRUTH, in LAW.

Appendix F: Updates creating the 2nd Edition

These updates are discussed in the order in which I find the easiest to explain. However, before that, a little background. First of all please note that the Magna Carta was a ***Treaty***. In other words, not any kind of 'Act of Parliament'/Legislation/Statute. (For the simple reason that 'Parliament' had not been invented at the time … that latter 'experiment in human relations' took another 80 or so years to evolve … probably as a method of subsuming the power of the Magna Carta).

Consequently when the Magna Carta refers to "the law of the land" it could only mean one possible thing: The Common Law … which it was attempting to document and set aright, for the first time in history.

Being a Treaty, the Magna Carta was a binding Agreement between the Monarchy of England, Ireland and France … and The People of England, Ireland and France. And can thus only ever be annulled by the full consent of both Parties to the Treaty. (I've never given my consent to waive any of its terms & conditions … have you?)

So it is possible to look at this Treaty and to determine what is necessary for the application of the Common Law. Reading it, one sees references to: Archbishops, Bishops, Abbots, Earls, Barons, Knights, Justiciars (Justices), Foresters, Sheriffs, Stewards, Bailiffs and Constables. And 'good men of the neighbourhood'. And 'a Jury of one's peers', of course.

Conspicuous, by their absence, are: Judges (unless one assumes a Justiciar is a Judge … but that is actually not, precisely, what a Justiciar was), Lawyers, Attorneys, Barristers, Magistrates, Solicitors and (of course) Politicians.

So there's a thought, is there not? Is it reasonable to conclude that such animals as these have, latterly, simply managed to carve a niche for themselves into the universal psyche? And that they all are, in reality, completely dispensable. Disposable. Supernumerary. (For all their 'puff', and self-aggrandised 'importance'?).

I suggest that the most likely answer is: *"Yes"*. I suggest that they have managed to create a fictional non-reality – within which they can swim – a Disneyland called 'Legalese' – and managed to elbow their way to the front of the psyche queue, by hook or by crook. ('Crook' being the operative word?).

A world where they can say, in Court: *"I have been instructed by my Client to tell you that … yada yada"* – which means that they, themselves, can never be held responsible for what they have said (even if it was, in fact, an outright lie). And that the buck has been passed to some amorphous 'Client' – who was not, of course, present at the time – such as to be questioned as to why the Representative is telling lies.

Oh, gosh, yes! This happens. It's the only way they can actually work. The oak panelling of a Courtroom seems to act as a kind of Faraday Cage, to make sure The Truth never filters through into the room itself.

Why is their world fictional? Because it is the world they feel they can create by 'simply writing something down'.

It goes like this. What happened was: In 1215 those, at the time, looked around, observed what they saw, and wrote down how to apply 'justice', based on observations and experiences. They took reality, and wrote it down.

The 'Legalese' world works the opposite way round. The Legislators simply write down whatever they decide … ***and assume that creates reality***. If they need to adjust the meanings of words, that's no barrier. They just do it, which is why they require Law Dictionaries. It's the same attitude that a small child has, when being scolded, when they close their eyes to 'make the parent disappear'. And, to their chagrin, the parent is still there, still telling them off, when the child opens its eyes again.

Reality is reality. You can't write what you want. You can only observe what is … and write up what you see. Only the Walt Disneys of this world could write what they wanted everyone to see - in order to depict fairytales.

And here's the 'cruncher'. You can read Statute after Statute. And they will document, in excruciating detail, every which-way of rules and regulations to be followed (creating reality using their pens). But, somewhere, in each Statute, you'll find a small section that says: *"Any and all of these rules are subject to the Judge's discretion"*.

And there you have it: The Universal Getout Clause, which translates as: *"We tried to define it all, but reality will always catch up with us, so we will always defer to the Judge, at the time of making the decision"*.

And that Universal Getout Clause provides each Judge with a Road to Tyranny. Because it means that 'anything they say … goes'.

Or, at least it would, if the individual using that road was, in fact, a Judge. Fortunately (for all of us) they are not. Not a Judge. And therefore can't use that Road to Tyranny.

But you need to know how and why that is. ***And you need to be prepared to tell them why they are not a Judge. And they won't like it. They. Don't. Like. It. Up 'em.***

We'll get to all this.

Don't run ahead. Don't jump ahead. If you skip the basics, and don't fully understand what you are doing, they will rip your head off. They have had centuries to perfect their witchcraft and 'magic'.

Sheriffs.

The Sheriff was, and is, a 'shire reeve'. Someone who could write. (Remember: The whole of history is all about those few who could write, taking the piss out of the majority who could not). The idea was that he was the King's Man, in charge of a County. His job was threefold: (a) Collect taxes, (b) Keep the peace in the Shire, (c) Collect more taxes. Occasionally he would have a fourth role, which would be (d) Collect even more more taxes.

Now, 'taxes' = 'money'. And elsewhere in this book you will find chapter and verse as to why 'money' is an illusion. And the Common Law is all about reality, not illusion.

So, if you remove the illusions from the Sheriff's job, to get to his REAL job, it comes down to 'keeping the peace in the Shire'. And a 'peaceful Shire' is one where people don't kill each other. (Which is quite important because, when the King decided to fight a war, he would need an Army … and would need people alive in the Shires in order to form his Army! See? That's how their minds work! You thought they kept you alive because they loved you? Wrong! They keep you alive because they may need cannon fodder, matey! Don't ever kid yourself, sunshine!)

Now, one of the important things a Sheriff did was to take an Oath of Office. Well, two, actually. First of all he would have to swear, on pain of death, allegiance to the King. Such as become the King's Man. And then he would have to swear allegiance to the population of the Shire (so that he could ensure there was sufficient able-bodied men, whenever an Army was required).

Now, go back to that time. These Oaths were sworn under the Common Law. The Law-of-the-Land.

Judges (and Magistrates).

Now, fast forward to recent times. There are, actually, still a few High Sheriffs about. And certainly in Scotland and Ireland, where they can be found in relative abundance.

However, their role has been spread out, and morphed into 'moveable' Judges. Whereby 'the Shire' no longer has the importance it once had … the whole Nation (or Nations) now assuming that importance, with Judges moving around on 'circuits', and so on.

(Claiming independence from Parliament, but their 'boss', the Lord Chancellor, being appointed by Politicians? Errrm: *"Appointed by the Sovereign, upon advice from the Prime Minister"*. Yes, methinks that spells 'political' … what about you?)

But the Oaths of Office are similar to Sheriffs … to the point of being the same for all intents and purposes. Here they are:

"I, ________, do swear by Almighty God that I will be faithful and bear true allegiance to Her Majesty Queen Elizabeth the Second, her heirs and successors, according to law. "

And:

"I, ________, do swear by Almighty God that I will well and truly serve our Sovereign Lady Queen Elizabeth the Second in the office of ________, and I will do right to all manner of people after the laws and usages of this realm, without fear or favour, affection or ill will. "

Geez! **"… do right to all manner of people after the laws and usages of this realm, without fear or favour, affection or ill-will"**!!! Holy Black's Law Dictionaries, Batman!

And notice, it says "laws" and not "legals"!

Yes, it's an Oath sworn in accordance with the Common Law. An Oath sworn to serve & protect. To serve and protect **"… all manner of people"**.

Now: Where does it say, in those Oaths of Office, that a Judge has the right to make any decisions? The right (for example) to decide that the keys of one's home should be handed to some amorphous CORPORATION? I don't see that there anywhere.

(Let's face it … the keys to the Judge's home are not on the table, are they?)

And, going back to the Common Law, what it says is that the Judge is swearing to simply guide/support the Common Law **" … without fear**

or favour", on the basis that the Common Law itself attempts to **"... do right to all manner of people"**.

Or, in a nutshell, to run a Court de jure properly. If any 'decisions' are required, they are limited to the admissibility (or not) of the evidence presented to the Jury.

I think you'll find we have now discovered the true job of a Judge, have we not?

Well, from experience, you'll discover that the answer is: *"Yes"*. Because, if you carry on reading, you'll discover how they can be tied up in knots whenever they try to step out of that very limited role (as they do ... frequently).

We can do this by considering the Courts de facto.

Where there is no Jury to do the decision-making.

In a Court de facto the Judge purports to do all the decision-making.

But that's not any part of his Oath of Office.

So, what's going on?

What is going on is, simply, a con-trick.

It goes like this. Someone takes the Judicial Oaths of Office and can, therefore, call themselves a Judge, and run Courts de jure. Acting, basically, as an Umpire.

But, because they can call themselves a Judge, they can be hired to run Courts de facto.

However, while running a Court de facto, ***they cannot be acting under their Oath of Office***. The very Oath that enables them to call themselves 'a Judge'. BECAUSE IT IS NOT A COMMON LAW COURT. Thus, when attempting 'decision-making' in a Court de facto, ***they are impersonating a Judge***.

And, as a 'Judge-impersonator', they have absolutely no right whatsoever to firstly run the proceedings, nor to make any orders, nor to make any decisions. They have no more right to do that than anyone else on the planet.

Courts de jure are very rare. They tend to be High Courts, large enough (and kitted out) for Juries.

Whereas Courts de facto can be found in abundance, from the lowest Magistrate's Court to the County Courts. Almost everything "legal" is processed via Courts de facto these days.

So, if you have understood the forgoing, your remedy in LAW, for just about everything is: ***"Ask them whether or not they are acting under their Oath of Office at the time"***.

The results of this question can range from the 'stunning' to the 'spectacular'.

The likelihood will be a long bout of silence in the Court. (Some Magistrates – who haven't the faintest idea what is going on – may naively answer: *"Yes"* – but thus far we have never had a *"Yes"* from 'much more knowledgeable' Judge-impersonators).

The follow-up to any *"Yes"* answer would be (never tried it, because we have never had a *"Yes"*) – but it would be: *"Repeat it for me,* ***verbatim****, and we will discuss it"*. (This could be why we have never had a *"Yes"*?)

It is more likely that the initial response will be either 'silence', or: *"I don't need/choose to answer that!"*. To which the answer is, of course: *"Oh yes you do. Because unless you confirm you are acting under your Oath of Office, then you are simply impersonating a Judge, and have no right whatsoever to be sitting where you are sitting, and attempting to run any proceedings – let alone make any decision or orders. You do understand that, don't you? I certainly do"*.

If the Judge-impersonator makes any attempt to continue, then you can say: *"Any order you make which does* ***not*** *contain a sworn declaration,* ***from you****, that you were* ***acting under your Oath*** *at the time of making the decision, will* ***not*** *be lawfully binding upon me, and I shall ignore it. I will write back to the Court accordingly. Good day sir/madam"*.

Get up and leave. The order will ***not*** contain that sworn declaration.

(From the best of our experience) It is likely that s/he would be fired as a 'Judge', if it did.

If you do receive an Order from the Hearing you can send it back saying: *"There is no confirmation that Mr/Mrs. XXXX was acting under their Oath of Office at the time of making this Order. Amend it accordingly with their Confirmation Signature such as to make it LAWFULLY binding, before sending it back to me. Until then, this Order is not properly made nor served. Do not attempt to serve me any further Orders that are not so confirmed"*.

Note: ALWAYS have a friend with you in Court. Someone who would be prepared to write a Statement of Truth (affidavit) about what they observed.

Updates creating the 2nd Edition

Bailiffs.

Returning to the time when the Sheriff was in charge of a Shire, the area was divided up into Bailiwicks. And to each Bailiwick was allocated a Bailiff. Yet another sub-King's Man, who also took an Oath of Office. Thus the job description of a Bailiff is simply that of an underling to a Sheriff.

Or, in these times, a Judge. But, once again, Bailiffs are no longer restricted to a specific area.

Nevertheless, like Sheriffs and Judges (and Magistrates) they are still PUBLIC SERVANTS. And, therefore, as a Member of the Public, ***you are their Master/Mistress***.

And, in the same way that you can fire/sack a Judge-impersonator, so you can also fire/sack a Bailiff: *"Services not required"*. (Yes, I've done this on several occasions now).

This biggest problem, of course, is that these Organic Robots are the 'muscle' used to intimidate you, and have no knowledge of what is really going on. All they have is 'a piece of paper' on which 'a Warrant' is printed. They have no idea (nor want any idea) that the Warrant is totally unlawful (or even what that means), and that the piece of paper is worth nothing more than toilet paper.

Consequently they are not interested in 'dialogue', generally having no means of entering into any such dialogue.

For these reasons they need to be handled in a different way. There are two (possibly three) ways available. The first is obvious: A group of friends barring the way. Allied to this, but at the same time distinct from it, is a thing called 'Common Assault'. Bailiffs may very well have heard of Common Assault, but probably do not know what it actually means. Most people think that 'assault' must be physical (in some way or other). This is not true. The definition of Common Assault 'anything that even makes one feel unsafe – i.e. afraid for their safety'. This includes someone moving towards you in a 'threatening manner'. Or taking some action that is 'threatening'.

Consequently, a Bailiff approaching friends in a threatening manner, or making threats against them, is Common Assault. (It might be hard to argue the same for you, if your Name is on a Warrant, but it is perfectly possible to argue assault on someone who is simply sitting quietly on your doorstep, in an otherwise peaceful manner).

Furthermore, if there is anyone else in your home at the time (children for instance), who are made to 'feel afraid' by (say) 'loud banging on the door', then they have been assaulted.

So you can use Common Assault to the maximum ... and that includes any threats to (say): *"Come back with a Policyman"*.

Remember: Common Assault is a Human-to-Human thing. It has nothing to do with "legal" and everything to do with "lawful". If they have 'lawful excuse' to take you out – that's one thing – but they cannot have any excuse whatsoever for 'taking someone else' – even by 'accident'.

So Common Assault is the second thing, and should be used to the maximum.

The third is more complicated. It's called a Commercial Lien.

Do not make the mistake of thinking that – because it has 'Commercial' in the title – it is a part of 'Commercial' (namely 'Admiralty') Law. It isn't. It is the Human-to-Human remedy provided by the Common Law.

And it works entirely between Human Beings. If you have been 'wronged' by some other Human Being, then you can claim lawful remedy – which generally amounts to a large claim of 'money' (which they still believe in) against them. This 'money' being the 'lien' part.

Let's just step back a bit. The Bailiff will (these days) be the Employee of some CORPORATION. A Limited Company. His 'liability', ***to the Company***, may very well be 'limited to his shareholding or to his employ'.

However, his 'liability' to other Human Beings is, at all times, UNLIMITED. Something he will have forgotten (or will not even know).

However, at the Nuremberg Trials, following World War II, it was re-iterated in large letters, to all and sundry: EVERYONE IS INDIVIDUALLY RESPONSIBLE FOR THEIR OWN ACTIONS. (*"I was only obeying orders"* is not any defence, in LAW).

And there's no escaping that, no matter what uniform one wears, and no matter what role or capacity one is acting under.

From out of the Common Law comes the Commercial Lien. And the only time a Court would be necessary – would be ***to remove*** such a Lien. It can be applied without requiring any Court Hearing or 'official judgement'.

Updates creating the 2nd Edition

It revolves around the inescapable fact that, if an individual has been 'wronged', then only that individual has first-hand knowledge of the 'wrong'. It also revolves around the maxim that *'An unrebutted Statement stands as the Truth, in Law'*, and that (consequently) *'An unrebutted Statement of Truth stands as a Judgement, in Law'*.

'Unrebutted' is the key thing here. A rebutted Statement fails. A Statement only stands ***if not rebutted***. (It stands by acquiescence, or by tacit acceptance). So the other Party must be given every chance to rebut, in order that you remain in good faith.

Thus all that is necessary is to write those Statements of the Truth as you see it, as a witnessed affidavit. (The Witness merely witnessing your Signature against the Statements i.e. *"Yes, I know this individual, and it was s/he who made the Signature on the main document. I vouch for the fact that s/he made that Signature in my presence"*). (The Witness does not need to know, nor understand, those actual Statements made).

This Statement of Truth is then sent to whomsoever 'wronged' you, saying *"I believe this is what you did to me. I have listed out your actions point by point. I intend to place this on the Public Record, unless you can, WITH EVIDENCE, disprove any of the Statements I have made. You have 30 days to do that. Whatever remains unrebutted will be placed on the Public Record, and I will leave it there for all to see, including the Credit Reference Agencies who will be notified accordingly. Your actions against me can only be remedied by payment of £XXXX to myself. Upon such payment I will remove the exposure from the Public Record"*.

You would point out that such a Lien cannot be touched, in any way, by any Judge. This must be so, because only you have the first-hand knowledge of what occurred. Only a Jury of 12 can remove, or reduce, or modify, such a Common Law Lien … after listening to, and hearing statements from, both sides.

An example (from one of mine) is:

Statement of Truth

I, Veronica: of the Chapman family (as commonly called), being the Undersigned, do solemnly swear, declare, and depose:

1. THAT I am competent to state the matters set forth herein.

2. THAT I have first-hand knowledge of the facts stated herein.

3. THAT all the facts stated herein are true, correct, and certain, admissible as evidence, and if called upon as a witness, I will testify to their veracity.

4. THAT the eternal, unchanged principles of Commercial Law are:

a) A workman is worthy of his hire.

b) All are equal under the Law.

c) In Law, truth is sovereign.

d) Truth is expressed in the form of an affidavit.

e) An unrebutted affidavit stands as truth in Law.

f) An unrebutted affidavit becomes the judgment in Law.

g) All matters must be expressed to be resolved.

h) He who leaves the battlefield first loses by default.

i) Sacrifice is the measure of credibility.

j) A lien or claim can be satisfied only through an affidavit by a point-for-point rebuttal, resolution by jury or payment.

5. THAT Commercial processes (including this Affidavit and the required responses to it) ARE NON-JUDICIAL and pre-judicial because:

a) No judge, court, government or any agencies thereof, or any other third parties whatsoever, can abrogate anyone's Affidavit of Truth; and

b) Only a party affected by an affidavit can speak and act for himself and is solely responsible for responding with his own Affidavit of Truth, which no one else can do for him.

6. THAT the lawful seizure, collection, and transfer of ownership of money or property must be effected by means of a valid Commercial Lien.

7. THAT I am not the creation or chattel property of any person or any government agency whatsoever. I am not under any obligation whatsoever to any governmental agency, state or federal (i.e. union), or any of their self-passed laws, statutes, regulations or policies.

8. THAT any and all of the various papers, documents, adhesion contracts, or "agreements" I may have signed with any government agency or entity or any others that might be construed to indicate a conclusion contrary to my herein-below assertions were made, signed by me on the basis of mistake due to lack of full disclosure creating a deliberate lack of full knowledge, a deliberate action of fraud, non-disclosure, concealment of material fact, and misrepresentation. Such action thereby creates a stressful situation of duress and intimidation, vitiating all documents by such action of fraud.

9. THAT it is the sincerest belief and spiritual conviction of this Affiant that slavery and peonage are immoral, are violations of the First Precept of Commercial Law ("a workman is worthy of his hire"), that fraud, misrepresentation, nondisclosure, intimidation, deceit, concealment of material fact, lying, and treachery are morally wrong.

10. THAT I have absolutely no desire whatsoever to be a "client" (slave) of any governmental agency, state or federal (i.e. union), or any of their Principals, or the "United Kingdom," or to incur any debts or obligations to said entities for whatever "benefits" said entities might purpose to provide or seek to provide to this Affiant, or be directed by, subject to, or accountable to any parties other than my own conscience and best judgement for the purpose of preserving inviolate my unalienable/inalienable indefeasible rights to life, liberty, freedom and property while engaging in the honourable, productive, and non-harmful activities of my life.

11. THAT I, Veronica: of the Chapman family, am the sole and absolute owner of myself, my body, and my

estate, and possess unconditional, allodial, sovereign title thereto, and that I abjure, renounce, forsake, and disavow utterly and absolutely now and forever all presumptions of power, authority, or right by any governmental agency, its Principals, over the rights, life, liberty, freedom or property of this Affiant from whatever source presumed or derived.

12. … and so on … listing precisely who they are and what they did. As many points as necessary …

CONTRACT OF LIABILITY FOR ALLEGATIONS

(Note: Renumber accordingly below … and don't include this reminder! I apologise to those Readers with a brain, but you wouldn't understand why I had to write that last sentence …)

??. THAT if the Undersigned had failed to rebut such claims or charges, the Respondent would have immediately declared a default against the Undersigned and proceeded to collect on the claims made as being in agreement with said claims or charges. The Respondents having made the claim or charge against the Undersigned, thereby creating an implied contract, the Undersigned having rebutted said claim or charge demanding proof of said implied contract, a true binding contract was thereby created.

??. THAT the Respondents' attacks on the commercial or private liability of the Undersigned Affiant, and this Affidavit or response/rebuttal to said claims or charges, created the mutually voluntary, consensual, commercial, private contract by and between the Undersigned and Respondents. Failure of Respondents to prove their claims or charges against the Undersigned within thirty (30) days (or in the alternative cease all collection or enforcement actions against the Undersigned, including a written apology) shall constitute deliberate criminal actions and wilful breach of and default on a bilateral contract (Affidavit of Agreement) formed knowingly, intentionally, and voluntarily by and between the Undersigned and the Respondents.

??. THAT only I, the Human Being involved against my free will in this instant matter, can determine how much stress, harassment, and other disturbance I have suffered to my day-to-day existence (Enclosure A is a typical example), and consequently only I am in the position of decide and dictate my desired compensation, being the amount of £100,000 (one hundred thousand pounds sterling) for all combined attempts to trespass on my absolute sovereignty, that being the sum total demanded by this Commercial Lien on each of the named Respondents.

??. THAT by specifically offering Xxx Company Limited the chance to apologise in writing (although the opportunity has always been there for the taking) via a **Notice and Demand**, signed for by Xxx Company Limited on 10th June, 2010 in this instant matter (Enclosure B is Proof of Delivery), I come to this position with clean hands as having shown good faith.

??. THAT for all the purposes of all of the forgoing, all references to "Xxx Company Limited" shall be construed to refer to individuals who consider their Legal Fiction Names to be Aaa Bbb, Ccc Ddd and Eee Fff, and who list their address as c/o Xxx Company Limited, ? Street, ?, Middlesex [postcode].

??. THAT I, Veronica: of the Chapman family, the Undersigned Affiant, depose and certify that I have written the foregoing with intent and understanding of purpose, and believe the statements, allegations, demands and contents herein to be true, correct, and complete, commercially reasonable, and just, to the best of my knowledge and belief.

Signed Sealed and delivered:

Witnessed by:

DO NOT WRITE ONE OF THESE LIGHTLY. IF YOU MAKE A FALSE STATEMENT, IT IS PERJURY. IF YOU DO NOT FULLY UNDERSTAND WHAT IT SAYS AND MEANS, OR CANNOT PROVE (IF NECESSARY) EVERYTHING YOU SAY … DON'T DO IT!

So, point out to a Bailiff that he could easily end up with a Commercial Lien up his jacksey, and tell him to go find out what that is … before taking one more breath.

"I wouldn't worry about that bit of toilet paper you have in your grubby mitt, mate! If I were you I'd be a darn sight more worried about the fact I can take your house off you! Right. What's your Name? And I want a Service Address for you … show me your Warrant Card …"

Furthermore we have had success with a **Notice of Removal of Implied Right of Access**, on a front door.

Here's an example:

To all it concerns

NOTICE TO AGENT IS NOTICE TO PRINCIPAL AND NOTICE TO PRINCIPAL IS NOTICE TO AGENT APPLIES

Notice of Removal of Implied Right of Access

You are advised to read the following notice thoroughly and carefully. It is a lawful notice. It informs you. It means what it says.

I hereby give notice that the implied right of access to the property known as <address> [postcode], and surrounding areas, has been removed, along with all associated property including, but not limited to, any private conveyance in respect of the following:

1) ANY employee, principal, agent, third party or representative or any other person acting on behalf of or under the instruction of HER MAJESTYS COURT SERVICE, or any other CORPORATE BODY (i.e. Company) howsoever named and,

2) ANY POLICE OFFICER who is acting for the CORPORATE POLICE and NOT acting as a Constable for and on behalf of Her Majesty Queen Elizabeth II and her people as expressed in the Oath of Office of all POLICE men and women, that is as Public Servants, upon your Oath of Office to serve "with fairness, integrity, diligence and impartiality, upholding fundamental human rights and according equal respect to all people; and that I will, to the best of my power, cause the peace to be kept and preserved and prevent all offences against people and property"

COMMON LAW JURISDICTION APPLIES EXCLUSIVELY

Please also take notice that the land known as England is a Common Law jurisdiction and any transgression of this notice will be dealt with according to Common Law.

Any and all access to the above mentioned properties shall be by strict invitation only and shall be subject to terms and conditions, available by written request.

Updates creating the 2nd Edition

We do not have, and have never had, a contract. And any permission that you believe you may have from me is hereby withdrawn. If you believe that you have power of attorney to act on my behalf you are hereby fired, and any consent that you believe you may have, tacit or otherwise, is hereby withdrawn. If you feel so inclined as to enforce statutes as a consequence of this matter I will report your conduct to ALL relevant bodies and will pursue Proof of Claim in affidavit form, under your full commercial liability and under the penalty of perjury.

You are deemed to have been served this notice with immediate effect.

In sincerity and honour, without ill-will, frivolity, or vexation,

Veronica: of the Chapman family, as commonly known, English Sovereign.

Without any admission of any liability whosoever, and with all Indefeasible Rights reserved.

It also helps to have the Police Oath stuck in to the front door as well. (Just in case!)

"I, ... of ... do solemnly and sincerely declare and affirm that I will well and truly serve the Queen in the office of constable, with fairness, integrity, diligence and impartiality, upholding fundamental human rights and according equal respect to all people; and that I will, to the best of my power, cause the peace to be kept and preserved and prevent all offences against people and property; and that while I continue to hold the said office I will to the best of my skill and knowledge discharge all the duties thereof faithfully according to law."

Obviously you would want to 'discuss' this with them (before opening the door). Asking them if they understood what **"... fairness, integrity, diligence and impartiality"** means, and furthermore things like "**... upholding fundamental human rights**" … and: *"Where does it say upholding fundamental CORPORATE rights … it doesn't Constable …does it? No, it doesn't. So why are you hell bent on upholding Corporate rights, based on a Order made by someone who was simply IMPERSONATING a Judge at the time, against MY INDEFEASIBLE i.e. FUNDAMENTAL HUMAN RIGHTS?"* … and so on.

("Do you know how serious it is to IMPERSONATE a Police Constable? You do? Well, it is even more serious to impersonate a Judge!")

("What made you a Police Constable? It was your Oath wasn't it? Well, it's the same for a Judge. His Oath makes him a Judge. But if he doesn't act under it, then he's not a Judge …in the same way that – if you don't act under your Oath – you are

not a Policeman. When does it say – on that piece of paper – that the Judge was acting under his Oath at the time?")

And the Policyman's Oath finishes up by saying **"I will to the best of my skill and knowledge discharge all the duties thereof faithfully according to law."** ... and: *'Do you actually understand what that means, Constable? Well read the previous wording, it's all defined in the first bits. Just keep reading it all, until you finally 'get it'. It's all there. Just keep reading until you 'get' what 'law' actually is".*

Debt Collectors, including non-Court Bailiffs.

Well, these are easy-peasy. Simply because they do not have a leg to stand on, and it is very easy to explain.

The scenario will be that they write to you, demanding payment, and telling you they have obtained a Court Order against you, in the form of a Warrant.

Quite probably the Warrant will have been obtained without your knowledge. Usually (in the UK) they obtain their toilet paper Warrants from the Northampton Bulk Clearing Centre (part of the HER MAJESTY'S COURT SERVICES Corporation, which itself a sub-Company of the MINISTRY OF JUSTICE Corporation).

A Deputy District Judge will have 'sat' (shat?), and rubber-stamped the Warrant without even reading it. (This is proved by the fact that they can contain typing errors, spelling mistakes ... lack of material information, such as relevant Account Numbers, etc ... and yet the so-called Judge will be quite happy to wield the rubber-stamp).

What is a 'Deputy District Judge'? It is a 'glorified Solicitor' who 'trades as a Judge' between 5 and 15 days per year, probably for some extra bunce/pocket money (assuming they don't get enough by shafting their 'tricks' ... errrr I mean 'Clients').

Bailiffs and Debt Collectors turn up on your doorstep waving bits of paper signed by these dummies.

And they claim it all in the name of 'justice'.

But there's a problem.

It goes like this. If you knew someone was in 'debt', and offered to help them out, what would you do?

Well, if you were a reasonable individual, you'd contract them and say: *"Look, I can see you have a bit of trouble. Would you like me to pay it off for you?"*

Now, if they said: *"Yes"*, you'd have two choices. You could either just pay it off … and forget about it (write it off … parents often do that for their children), or you could say: *"Well, if I did pay it off for you … would you pay me back later?"*

Now, if they said: *"No, I won't pay you back"*, then you'd know the score, and probably would retire gracefully from the scene, and let them get on with their own problem. You offered to help, but they would not accept the terms.

However, if they said: *"Yes … I'll pay you back"*, it would be a different matter. Because they would have given an undertaking to you … they would have created an obligation to you. Would they not? So, if you went ahead and paid it off, you could quite rightly claim that they owed you, instead of the original, couldn't you?

Well, yes, you could.

But these are not the scenarios when Debt Collection Agencies are involved. ***They did not contact you first, to find out whether or not you considered you actually owed the 'money'. They did not arrange any obligation from you, such as to get your SIGNED agreement to pay them back.***

No, they just waltzed in, and started throwing their (imagined) weight around.

Pointing this out to them tends to shut them up. Although you might end up having to do it forcibly (you can start off politely asking for a copy of your Contract of Obligation to them but … as their demanding letters reach fever point … and very large fonts …), by writing (what one might call) a 'strong' letter. One that explains all this (in your own words, as necessary), and probably including such phrases as:

> *"Take me to Court, then. A REAL Court. One with a Jury. You tell them your side of the story, and I tell them mine. And if they find me guilty of wrongdoing, they will agree that a LAWFUL Warrant should be issued.*
>
> *You will tell them that I owe you some money, and I will explain to them exactly how you got YOURSELVES into that situation. By deviousness. By deception. By underhandedness. By FRAUD.*
>
> *I will explain it all to them, chapter & verse.*
>
> *What do you think they'll say?*
>
> *Do you think they will agree with you?*
>
> *If they do, then you'll have the LAWFUL Warrant you need.*

Or ... do you suppose - having heard the WHOLE story - they might - just might - say: "Well it would have been all right if you had established all this beforehand, and agreed to be paid back, and had expected to be reimbursed plus some reasonable costs ... but to just waltz in, uninvited, take over, and start flinging your weight around, isn't really on. Especially when you started to demand about 900% of your outlay. And, by the way, if YOU could buy it for 10% or less ... why was it not possible to directly sell it to the original person at that same price? Why was the original demand so high, if it could be sold at 10% or less? What special favour do you have, to buy it at 10% or less?" "

And, possibly including the paragraph:

"You are pig ignorant and arrogant, aren't you? Scrub your disgustingly filthy, dirty hands forever ... you'll never get them clean."

And so on.

(Well, that's what I do)

Societies and Statutes, etc.

If you are still having trouble understanding the Freeman Principles (see the other *Appendix* and relevant *Chapters*), then consider whether or not your Solicitor is bound by the Legislated Rules (Statutes) of the Medical Authority in your Country. And whether or not your Doctor is bound by the Legislated Rules of the Law Society in your Country. And whether or not your Postman is bound by either set of rules.

That's all it takes – in order to understand.

Mortgages

These were mentioned in First Edition. However much more information has since come to light.

Not least of which being information obtained directly from The Horse's Mouth, namely the Bank of England. Courtesy of someone who, at the time, would have been 'very much in the know'.

A certain Mr. Paul Tucker, and what he wrote in the Bank of England's First Quarterly Bulletin for 2008.

Who is Mr. Paul Tucker? Executive Director for Markets, and a Monetary Policy Committee Member - subsequently becoming Deputy Governor, Financial Stability at the Bank of England, and now, at the time of writing this update, being a Non-executive Financial Services Authority (FSA) Board Member.

What did he write? He said: ***"Subject only but crucially to confidence in their soundness, banks extend credit by simply increasing the borrowing customer's current account, which can be paid away to wherever the borrower wants by the bank 'writing a cheque on itself'. That is, banks extend credit by creating money."***

A source link to that bulletin is: http://www.bankofengland.co.uk/publications/quarterlybulletin/qb0801.pdf

Mr. Tucker's statements appear on Page 103 (PDF Page 105), bottom-left paragraph.

Holy Shit! Were we supposed to read that??? (Probably not!) ***"Banks extend credit by creating money???"***

They do this by ***"writing cheque to themselves???"***

Which is, of course, all just another way of saying: *"Banks create money out of thin air"*. (And the rest of this book explains exactly how and why that must be. ***Because there is no other way***)

I think we can safely say that this 'writing cheques to themselves mechanism' occurs in accordance with factors such as 'credit worthiness' and so on … and very much in accord with 'Fiscal Policy' as dictated by HM Treasury. (Otherwise why all the furore about 'bailouts', in the autumn of 2008?)

Now, let's add yet another factor to this. Let's find out what a Promissory Note is, shall we? Well, we discover that it is basically, some piece of paper, on which there is writing/printing. It has a Date from the Maker of the note. It has the Signature of the Maker. It specifies an Amount of the monetary illusion, and it also specifies the name of the Payee (which could be simply 'the Holder' … or 'the Bearer', in the case of banknotes).

Since the monetary illusion is utterly worthless, the Promissory Note is, in itself, utterly worthless.

And then, if we check the defining Statute for 'Cash', we see that one of the definitions is: 'Promissory Note'.

Well, I never! My giddy Aunt! Holy Relations, Batman!

So, this is saying that 'cash' = utterly worthless!

"And your point is, Caller?"

My point is that, when you take out a Mortgage, you create a Promissory Note. It spans more than one piece of paper, which means that it is not immediately easy to view it as such. Nevertheless it is a Promissory Note.

The pieces of paper are called the Title (or Mortgage) Deed, which contains the Date, the Payee, and Your Signature, and always refers to the Mortgage Offer – which is the thing that contains all the 'numbers' (Amounts) involved.

And this is very 'clever'. Because Your Signature and the Date and the Payee are maintained separately … like a blank cheque that is dated and signed by you. And it's the bit that says: *"I authorise the Bank to place a Charge on my property, which is there in case I'm naughty in the next 25 years, and decide not to cough up".*

But the whole, taken together – the Mortgage Deed PLUS the Mortgage Offer is a Promissory Note – which YOU issued – AND IT PAYS IN FULL … AT THAT TIME … FOR THE PROPERTY YOU ARE BUYING.

Yes … it is utterly worthless. Yes. But so are the banknotes. All Promissory Notes are utterly worthless … BECAUSE MONEY IS AN ILLUSION!!!!!

The only question is: ***Are YOUR Promissory Notes more or less utterly worthless than those utterly worthless Notes issued by the Bank of England?***

It's just a consideration in 'utter worthlessness'. How can anything be more utterly worthless than something that is utterly worthless?

So, why is there a Charge on your property?

GOOD QUESTION!

And why do you need to make monthly payments on your Mortgage – when you already paid in full at the time?

ANOTHER VERY GOOD QUESTION!

The answer to the both questions is: ***Only because you were thoroughly deceived. And remain being deceived for (generally) 25 years … while the Bank unjustly enriches itself at your expense … and laughs all the way to the …***

And this is how it works:

1. You make an Application for a mortgage.

2. 'Credit worthiness' checks will be made on both yourself and the property in question. Assume these succeed.

3. You will receive a Title Deed, ready for your signature, and also the Mortgage Offer.

4. ***Now note:*** YOU WILL BE TOLD NOT TO DATE THE TITLE DEED … but merely to sign it in front of a witness (who also signs it, but DOES NOT 'date' it). There are reasons for this, as you will discover, if you keep reading below.

5. You will not be expected to sign the Mortgage Offer, but will probably be expected to 'initial' each page - as having read and understood it.

6. You send all of this back. This is how the 'cheque' i.e. Promissory Note is created in distinct parts. Should it come to 'repossession', a Court de facto will only be interested in the Title Deed containing Your Signature, and 'have you kept up the payments?' … and absolutely nothing else. It will not want to know, or hear, about ANYTHING else!

7. But wait! When you signed and sent back the Title Deed you were saying: *"I authorise the so-called Lender to place a Charge on this property with the Land Registry".*

8. But – ***you didn't own the property when you made that signature!*** Did you? You were forced to sign that piece of paper because the so-called Lender had told you that nothing would go ahead until you did. If 'nothing had gone ahead', you would have had no mortgage … and never owned the property at all! At any time. And you certainly didn't 'own' it before you had 'bought' it!

9. So, when you sign the Title Deed, authorising a Charge on a property you don't actually own … ***you are committing a fraud!***

10. But … it's OK … ***you didn't 'date' it!*** So, what the so-called Lender actually has is 'authorisation' to create a Charge on 'a property you don't own', and it simply needs to be 'dated'. ***Which can only happen,***

without being fraudulent, once you actually own it. Once you've actually bought it. Once you've paid for it IN FULL … such that you, and you alone, have the Full Title to the property.

11. All that needs to happen is for your purchase to take place – then, once it IS your property – The Title Deed can be 'dated' accordingly! (By the so-called Lender … who now has it … and then it can be posted off to the Land Registry). At this time your authorisation is no longer fraudulent, it is a Charge in their favour, and can be freely submitted to the Land Registry.

12. Now … think back to the previous paragraph: *"All that needs to happen is for your purchase to take place …"* is another way of saying that the purchase ***must be able to take place <u>without</u> the Charge on the Title Deed having been implemented***. So, if your purchase can take place … such as the property becomes entirely YOURS … such that you can lawfully authorise a Charge … ***why do you need to authorise the Charge?*** It's YOUR property. It had to be … otherwise the Title Deed authorisation would remain fraudulent.

13. Why ever would someone allow - someone else - a Charge over them, or their property, without the need to? So – what was the 'need'? The 'need' was that the so-called Lender said: *"Nothing will go ahead unless you sign this"*. That's it! Simply had you by the short & curlys! Nothing else. Another way of saying it: *"You don't get to own and live in this property unless we get a Charge on it"*.

14. And what is the Charge? Jam. Pure jam, honey, marmalade … for the so-called Lender. ***IT HAD NO EFFECT ON YOUR ACTUAL ABILITY TO ACTUALLY MAKE THE PURCHASE … only that they placed it as a unilateral stumbling block into your path. Something to provide them with, jam, jam, jam, milk, honey, more jam … you name it! For something like 25 years. On the basis that – if you stop supplying the jam … we'll grab your house off you.***

Updates creating the 2nd Edition

15. Go back to the beginning: You paid, in full, to purchase the property by tendering the Promissory Note (which incorporated the Title Deed). You had absolutely no need to do anything else … except (perhaps) to pay the so-called Lender a reasonable Administration Fee for the facility of (shall we say) 'monetising' your Promissory Note. A couple of £grand would surely have sufficed for that … after all … all it involved was placing a few numbers on to the odd database.

16. In case you are still wondering … the so-called Lender inserts the date (or Tippexes over one you may have written, and re-writes the date), once they have juggled databases sufficiently to make you the Full Title Owner, by 'monetising' Your Signature as much as is necessary.

17. The whole process is entirely fraudulent, and one massive scam that has gone on unchecked for centuries. To have been told that you needed to authorise the Charge was nothing short of a corrupt deception.

At a Repossession Hearing (which will 'morph', at some point during the process, into a Possession Hearing … because the Bank or Building Society are 'taking possession' of something they never had … and therefore couldn't be RE-possessing …) only three questions will be relevant, as far as the Court de facto is concerned:

1. Are you the Defendant?

2. Did you sign the Title/Mortgage Deed (authorising the Charge)?

3. Have you kept up the payments, or has the Charge been triggered?

That's it. The so-called 'Judge' will not be interested in anything else.

The Bank or Building Society will present a 'statement' showing your payments … which will tail off into 'lack of payments' (being the reason for the Possession Hearing). This 'statement' will normally date from the first payment you made.

But hold on! Something happened BEFORE you made that first payment … didn't it? Didn't the Bank or Building Society do some other things? Like settle up, on your behalf, with the previous Owner? Like ***actually 'buy'*** the property on your behalf?

Where's the 'accounting' for that? The accounting that would show a massive 'hole' in their books, as the loan (they were supposed to have made) left their ledgers?

Yes … they provide 'accounting' … but they don't provide the Full Accounting. Such as would start by showing this massive 'hole' … which then slowly – month-by-month – is re-filled with your payments?

Well, you'd think they would, wouldn't you?

But they don't.

However, according to the Banker's Books Evidence Act 1879, they can be made to show the Full Accounting. IF YOU CAN GET THE COURT TO ORDER THE BANK TO DO SO. (There's always a catch … to Statutes!)

But that doesn't stop you quoting it.

And, since the Bank/Building Society are supposed to balance their books regularly, it is felt likely that any massive debit (to buy your property) would be balanced by some form of massive 'credit' … based in the Signed Agreement comprising your Promissory Note.

So, what can you do … assuming that you are currently keeping up with your payments? Well, in this case you are perfectly safe from so-called repossessions. And you can still write polite letters, for example a letter requesting: *"The Full Accounting such as defined by the Banker's Books Evidence Act 1879"*. Make sure that you specify the date for the 'accounting' to start ***as the day you posted back the Title Deed and Mortgage Offer***. Because 'just after that' is when the 'accounting' should have started.

And see what they write back (if anything!)

You don't have to make any suggestion about 'not paying them'. You can say: *"I just want it for completion of my records"*.

Other things you can ask them are:

1. Is it true that the Title/Mortgage Deed PLUS the Mortgage Offer constitute the Agreement? They will answer: *"Yes"*, so ask them to send you a copy. Check the Date and see that it is not in your handwriting. Then write back, asking them why the date is not in your handwriting, and who wrote it in? They will try to fob you off as 'standard procedure', so you ask

them the same questions again – pointing out that 'standard procedure' does not explain 'what is beginning to look a bit like fraud'. They will eventually have to tell you that the date could only have been inserted once you, yourself, had Full Title Ownership to your house. You can then write saying: *"If I had Full Title Ownership – such that I was empowered to sign and authorise the Charge – then why was the Charge subsequently necessary? Did I own the property outright … or did I not?"* Don't hold your breath for an answer. In fact, you'll be quite lucky to get responses up to that point.

And, if you don't get responses … you'll now know why, won't you?

2. Is it true that they are NOW the OWNERS of these Agreement documents? (They will answer: *"Yes"*. This means that they have a Duty of Care over these documents … that you ENTRUSTED to them. A Duty to keep them safe and secure. Such that you could 'have sight' of them upon reasonable request. And you could make that request. And they should be prepared to show you the original of the Title Deed … the thing that incriminates you at a Possession Hearing … but they appear ***not*** to be able to show ***originals*** of the Mortgage Offer. We surmise this is because they have on-sold it, but we have not – at this time – established absolute cast-iron proof. However we have established an immense reluctance, on their part, to provide 'sight' of the ***original*** Mortgage Offer. They always offer 'copies', and we are left to wonder why that should be. It may be that you would have initialled every page of the original Mortgage Offer … to indicate you had read it. You would ***not normally*** have actually signed it. Only the Title Deed is ***normally*** signed, and witnessed. You will normally see that the date on the original of this Title Deed is ***not*** in your handwriting … because you were asked not to fill it in … see above).

Just a few things you could safely do.

If you've cottoned on to this deception as explained, then one other thing you ***could*** do – but it would take guts and a thorough understanding – would be to write to the Bank or Building Society, saying *"Get your fraudulent Charge off My Property. Right NOW. And then we can discuss how you refund everything I have paid you monthly, plus interest. We can discuss a reasonable Administration Fee you can keep, for the facility of monetising My Signature. Perhaps something like £2,000 might be reasonable. I* *will be writing to the Land Registry accordingly, pointing out that I consider your Charge to be fraudulent".*

And write the Land Registry, advising them that you have reason to believe the Charge to be fraudulent. (Tell them why - ***only if they ask*** – quite simply because they probably won't ask, or be interested in "Why?". That's not the Land Registry's main remit. However, if asked, you can say: *"Because I asked the Bank/Building Society to explain why the Charge was applied, and they have not been able to explain it to my satisfaction. If you want more information, try asking them yourselves. I'll be interested to know what they say"*).

Sovereignty

This is what it ALL comes down to.

Your Sovereignty.

Your Sovereignty as a flesh and blood Human Being, with a living soul. Your Mind. Your Limbs. Everything about you.

And the knowledge that this is what you are, and that TRESPASS upon it is TREASON.

In the UK, we have been led to believe that there is only one 'sovereign' i.e. the Monarch at the time.

This is a fallacy, and is easily proved to be so. You simply need to ask yourself a few simple questions, the first one being: *"Where does the sovereignty of the Monarch come from?"*

And the answer to that is pretty simple: *"From the Coronation Oath".*

And what was the Coronation Oath? The answer to that is: It was a binding Contract between the (in the most recent case) 'eldest daughter of the late King', and The People of the Nation. A Solemn Contract whereby she agreed to ***protect*** our customs and traditions (and our borders), and – in exchange – The People granted her 'the necessary sovereignty' to do just that. Via various 'Royal Prerogatives' (which she has never used in order to actually protect us in accordance with her Oath. But, for the purposes of this discussion, we'll put that aspect to one side. Fundamentally, if she doesn't protect us, then we have to protect ourselves, don't we?).

And it is not possible to grant (or 'give') something you, yourself, do not possess. Thus if The People granted her 'sovereignty', then The People must be 'sovereign' themselves.

Updates creating the 2nd Edition

In the same way that Politicians will talk about 'the sovereignty of Parliament'. Well, where does that come from? Who actually elects them? (Answers on a postcard).

I repeat: ***You cannot give something you, yourself, do not possess.*** (If I only have one apple, I can't give you two apples … I can only give you one apple, n'est-ce pas? And I certainly can't give you an orange, by the way).

So, it's all very simple. If the Monarch is Sovereign, then so must be each and every Member of The People. Because that's the only 'where' it can ever come from.

Therefore, it all comes down to 'getting your Mindset right', doesn't it?

This is surely just another way of expressing my Very Cunning 2-Step Plan for Freedom, is it not? After all, that's just saying: *"Get your Mindset right"*.

I might point out, at this juncture, that 'understanding the Sovereignty Issue' was precisely what the Irish were forced to do in 1916. Such that, in 1919, the Irish Free State (Eire) was created - based on the 1916 Declaration that every Irishman and Irishwoman was a Sovereign.

The Sovereignty Issue is key. It means that you are Supreme. (And, of course, so is everyone else). But it translates as: *"No-one is 'above' you …and everyone is equal at all times … consequently you can only ever EXTEND them the AUTHORITY to take away your Indefeasible Rights … and to bow before them"*. That's the fundamental key. Another way of expressing it is: *"By CONSENT"*… and here we have come full circle, back to what is said elsewhere this book.

(And, don't forget the fundamentals, and the big difference between AUTHORITY and RESPONSIBILITY: 'Authority' can be ***delegated***; 'Responsibility' can only ever be ***shared***).

So let's tie up the loose ends, shall we?

If everyone is Sovereign, then so are Judges, Magistrates, Bailiffs … and Policymen (and Politicians, etc.)

Yes … that's perfectly true … while they are NOT acting roles … in other words while they are simply their Human Selves (and not 'acting').

But when acting, their roles (as Judges, Magistrates, Bailiffs, etc) they are NOT Sovereigns … unless you choose to EXTEND them 'Dominion over your Sovereignty' ('bow before them'). Why? Because, when acting roles, they are PUBLIC SERVANTS. They are your SERVANTS, and you are their MASTER/MISTRESS.

Anything else is 'tail wagging the dog'.

So, they have a choice: Do they act in their roles, in accordance with their Oaths, which are to serve and protect your Sovereign Supremacy (certainly against all CORPORATE 'interests' … CORPORATIONS are not Human, and cannot possess Sovereignty) …

… or do they not?

If they chose 'not', then they are simply YOUR HUMAN SOVEREIGN EQUAL. Which means you are not superior to them, and they are not superior to you in any way, shape or form, and have no power ('dominion') over you at all. ***(No matter how much they may rant and rave)***.

Yes … this is a bit of a come-down for them … but they will just have to get used to it. They have ruled the roost for quite long enough, in the humble opinion of this Author.

We (in the UK) were born into a Constitutional Monarchy. In point of fact we need a Sovereign Republic, such as Eire. But we mustn't make the same mistakes as other Republics such as Eire, France, and the States of America (united). The mistake they have all made is to forget about the 'eternal vigilance' … vigilance that is essential to maintain any system in good working order.

Based on the Irish Declaration 1916, I offer this Declaration to all Englishmen and Englishwomen. The Scots and the Welsh need to create their own (via Cut/Paste? Ulster? Look 'south'!). I offer this before the ability to be English, Welsh, or Scottish becomes as thing of the past:

Updates creating the 2nd Edition

Declaration of a Sovereign English Republic for the People of England

ENGLISHMEN AND ENGLISHWOMEN: In the name of dead generations from which she receives her old traditions of nationhood, England, through you, summons all to her, and strikes for her freedom.

She declares the right of her people to the ownership of her, as England, and the unfettered control of English destinies to be sovereign and indefeasible. The usurpation of that right, by foreign people and government, has not extinguished it, nor can it ever be extinguished except by the destruction of the English people themselves.

Standing on these fundamental rights, and ever asserting them, it is hereby proclaimed a Sovereign English Republic as a Sovereign Independent Nation, and we pledge our lives in the cause of its freedom and its welfare, and its equality of status among nations.

The sovereignty of a Nation can only derive from the sovereignty of the people. This Sovereign Republic is entitled to, and claims the allegiance of, every sovereign Englishman and Englishwoman. In doing so, it guarantees all freedoms commensurate with peaceful co-existence among the people within its borders, and equal rights and opportunities to all who therein dwell. It declares its resolve to pursue the happiness and freedom of the whole nation and all of its parts, cherishing the children of the nation equally, and oblivious to the differences carefully fostered by foreign usurpers, who have sought to conquer by division, in the past.

From the customs and traditions of our forefathers comes the Common Law, which ensures peaceful co-existence, and brings with it the methods by which it can be applied in fair, honourable, and equitable ways in the true pursuit of Justice. Should any further governance be necessary, this shall only ever be obtained by decree from, and based on, and regularly renewed from, the indefeasibly assured sovereignty of every Englishman and Englishwoman.

As a Sovereign Republic, governance can only be affected by a 2/3rds majority vote of all people dwelling herein. This 2/3rds will thereby consent to be bound in honour by the terms of the vote. Those who do not vote affirmatively remain sovereign, and have thereby not extended consent. In this position they remain bound solely by the Common Law, and unbound by the terms of the governance vote. Only in this manner can governance occur, while sovereignty be still assured.

Authority

We are familiar with those who consider they are "the Authority", "in Authority", or work for "the Authorities", etc. What tends to be forgotten is that, by its nature, and by its very definition, 'authority' must be EXTENDED in order for it to have any effect.

It must be GIVEN. It CANNOT be just 'taken' or 'assumed' because that is not what it is. ('Authority' taken via the barrel of a gun' is a CRIME of TRESPASS against the SOVEREIGNTY of an individual).

For the simple reason that a Human operates by free will. In order to operate in accordance with 'directives' from some 'authority' (i.e. 'someone else'), then the Human's free will MUST be accepting the will of that someone else. This can only occur if the Human decides to accept the will of someone else.

Accepting and abiding by the will of someone else is the same as saying that the Human EXTENDS AUTHORITY to that someone else.

But, if a Human has free will, then that Human does not need to extend authority to anyone else.

And, if a Human does not have free will, then that Human is a robot. (And, therefore, is not Human after all).

What has happened is the attitude of 'safety in numbers' has become ingrained into the public psyche. As in: *"If I do what everyone else does, then I won't be picked upon … they'll leave me alone"*.

Which works fine … up to a point. It works fine until they start picking on you ... even though you've only ever "done what everyone else does".

And they start picking on you … and everyone else … because you have extended them the authority to do so … you gave them an inch and (by their very natures) they took a mile.

And that's the risk that is ALWAYS run when a Human EXTENDS authority to any other Human.

Taking that mile is done very slowly & very carefully. (David Icke calls it "The Totalitarian Tiptoe").

When someone, assuming 'authority', may create some kind of Order, it is important to remember that they have no authority over you, unless you extend it to them. One way to establish this is to realise that 'the servicing of Orders' is chargeable. And that you can set the rate to charge.

Updates creating the 2nd Edition

Promises

A Contract is a PROMISE (usually a pair of mutually-dependent Promises) that the Law will enforce.

But, what is a promise?

A promise is something 'that can't be done there and then' ... and therefore has to be 'promised'. Promised for ***the future***.

If that 'something' can be done 'there and then' ... then it would be done (and 'got out of the way' – and life would go on) ... there is no need to promise

This ties in with the promise, made by the Bank of England, on all banknotes. The promise (to pay a 'sum', on demand) has to be made - because there is no such thing as that 'sum' ... thus the act cannot take place there and then ... and has to be promised for some unspecified time in the future. This is, of course, the exact equivalent of that pot of gold at the end of the rainbow!

Thus all notes of 'currency' (all 'legal tenders') are empty, worthless, meaningless, Promissory Notes (IOUs)

And (with thanks to Stefan Molyneaux) we also have the insight that: ***If Human "A" makes a promise to Human "B", Human "C" is not bound by that promise.***

This has enormous repercussions, because it means that NOTHING any Government or Parliament does is worth a candle. Any promises they may make (e.g. to the European Union) DO NOT BIND ANYONE ELSE ... except the specific Ministers who are making those promises.

No-one has the right to assume they can make promises on anyone else's behalf.

To say, or assume they have such a right, is to deny an individual's free will to make their own promises.

As in the case of 'permissions', if any individual claims this Promising-on-behalf-of-others Right for themselves, then the correct description of that individual is: "Arrogant hypocrite". Anyone who makes such a claim must have a Personality Disorder. The only exceptions are in the case of children, and certain, specific, business situations - for example Boss/Secretary - but here BOTH have CONSENTED to the arrangement.

Arbitration

Courts de facto, and Judge-impersonators, consider they are, basically, 'arbitrating disputes'. (In order to 'find' in favour of the CORPORATION - against the Human Being – as their 'overriding objective'. All the time attempting to maintain a veneer of 'justice'. But it simply doesn't work, as any Freeman, in such a Court, knows only too well).

Here's what 'arbitration' actually means.

It only takes place, *honourably*, ***when both Parties in dispute consent to a common Arbitrator***. They must both – of their own free will, without duress, and without deception – agree:

1. To use a common Arbitrator to hear the details of the dispute, and
2. To abide by the Arbitrator's judgment.

Unless both Parties agree to these terms, no Arbitrator has any authority whatsoever to create any judgment.

This is simply because of the nature of 'authority' – which has to be extended. It is only extended by means of (1) and (2), above. 'Authority' cannot be bought, sold, or otherwise assumed.

Otherwise the authority just simply does not exist. If it did, then 'authority via the barrel of a gun' would be acceptable practice, instead of being deplorable, dishonest, dishonourable and utterly despicable.

For (1) and (2) to occur, both parties *must trust* the common Arbitrator. If either Party does not fully trust the Arbitrator, then honourable arbitration cannot take place.

A Court which does not have BOTH Parties TRUST and CONSENT does not have any AUTHORITY to make any decision that is binding in the Common Law. It is simply operating (metaphorically) 'via the barrel of a gun', and thus acting in a deplorable, dishonest, dishonourable and utterly despicable manner.

The only exception to this is for a Common Law offence (i.e. NOT a 'dispute'), where an Accused is heard by Jury of 12. And where the Jury returns a verdict based solely on the Common Law (as opposed to a form of 'single-person judgment').

If, by the refusal of one Party or the other to participate in the Arbitration of any dispute, the dispute remains unresolved, then there is nothing wrong with that. Both Parties are perfectly capable of agreeing, in a perfectly civilised manner, never to interact with each other ever again. If one Party feels 'aggrieved', then it should remember that we all feel aggrieved at various times in our lives. And that we learn by our mistaken alliances.

Arbitration (or Adjudication, if one prefers the term) without AUTHORITY is directly akin to the following scenario.

You are walking past the door of a Restaurant. As you do so, two Robots (with pointed heads, or flat-caps, wearing blue cloth, covered in chrome Masonic Regalia), grab you, handcuff you, and drag you inside. You are thrust into a chair, in front of a table, and a plateful of cat food is placed in front of you. You are told to eat it. You are then told you must pay £4,000 for this privilege, or face being jailed.

That is the equivalent to Arbitration without (1) and (2), above.

www.ingramcontent.com/pod-product-compliance
Lightning Source LLC
LaVergne TN
LVHW022333150926
848178LV00047B/1037